W9-BNB-135

UNITED METHODIST WORSHIP

UNITED METHODIST WORSHIP

Hoyt L. Hickman

ABINGDON PRESS
Nashville

UNITED METHODIST WORSHIP

Copyright © 1991 by Abingdon Press

All rights reserved.
No part of this work may be reproduced or transmitted in any
form or by any means, electronic or mechanical, including
photocopying and recording, or by any information storage or
retrieval system, except as may be expressly permitted by the
1976 Copyright Act or in writing from the publisher. Requests for
permission should be addressed in writing to Abingdon Press,
201 Eighth Avenue South, Nashville, TN 37203.

This book is printed on recycled, acid-free paper.

Library of Congress Cataloging-in-Publication Data

Hickman, Hoyt L. (Hoyt Leon), 1927–
    United Methodist worship / Hoyt L. Hickman.
      p.   cm.
    ISBN 0-687-43196-4 (alk. paper)
    1. United Methodist Church (U.S.)—Liturgy. 2. Methodist Church—
Liturgy. 3. Public worship. I. Title.
    BX8337.H54   1991
264'.076—dc   91-14641

Unless otherwise noted all Scripture quotations are from the New Revised
Standard Version of the Bible, copyright 1990 by the Division of Christian
Education of the National Council of Churches of Christ in the U.S.A.
    Those noted TEV are from the Bible in Today's English Version—Old
Testament: Copyright American Bible Society 1976; New Testament:
Copyright American Bible Society 1966, 1971, 1976.

MANUFACTURED IN THE UNITED STATES OF AMERICA

Contents

CHAPTER 1

Let's Go to Church

See You in Church Sunday

So you want to learn more about United Methodist worship.

You may be new to The United Methodist Church. You may be accustomed to worship in some other denomination, or you may be new to the experience of Christian worship.

You may have worshiped in a United Methodist Church all your life and still have many questions. You may have found a confusing variety of worship styles as you have gone from one United Methodist congregation to another. You may remember when worship in your church was very different from what it is now. You may have wondered about many practices, or taken them for granted, or never understood them.

This is not a book for pastors and others who plan and lead worship; it is for worshipers like you who want to worship week after week with more understanding about your local church.

Let's imagine that we're going to a typical worship service in your church, that this book is like a tour guide, and that from time to time we can stop the action long enough to explain what needs to be explained. Sometimes it will be helpful to flashback into biblical and church history.

If we're going to attend a service at your church, we need

to know when and where services are. Whatever the answer may be in your case, let's start with the fact that the overwhelming majority of Christian congregations worship every Sunday and ask: "Why Sunday? Why every week? Why do we have seven-day weeks anyway?"

We got our seven-day week from ancient Israel, where the Jews after they had labored six days, were commanded to observe every seventh day as the Sabbath, a holy day recalling how God rested on the seventh day of creation (Exodus 20:8-11; Deuteronomy 5:12-15). They referred to the days of the week as the first day, the second day, and so on. As other people in the Roman Empire and later in northern Europe adopted the seven-day week from the Jews, they named the days after heavenly bodies or gods—in English, Sunday, Mo(o)nday, and so on.

The early Christians met for worship on the first day of each week (Acts 20:7, 1 Corinthians 16:2), which they called "the Lord's Day" (Revelation 1:10) and which we call Sunday. The Lord's Day was a joyous celebration, recalling that Jesus had been raised from the dead and appeared to the disciples on the first day of the week (Matthew 28:1; Mark 16:2; Luke 24:1; John 20:1, 19). They also came to recall the first day of creation (Genesis 1:1-5); the eighth day of creation when, after resting on the seventh day (Genesis 2:2), God began to create anew; and the day of Pentecost seven weeks after Jesus' resurrection when the disciples were filled with the Holy Spirit and the Christian church was born (Acts 2).

When we worship on the Lord's Day, we, like the early Christians, are saying by our actions that on this "first day" we also can encounter the living Christ, can experience God's new creation, and can be filled with the Holy Spirit and renewed as the Christian church.

It is significant that we also usually worship on Sunday

morning. Early morning was the time of day when Jesus rose from the dead and when his disciples were filled with the Holy Spirit.

On the other hand, Christians since the earliest times have sometimes found it necessary or more convenient to hold their Lord's Day worship in the evening. Acts 20:7-11 describes a service held Saturday night, which was the first day of the week because the day begins at sunset in the Jewish and traditional Christian calendar. Today some congregations follow this tradition and hold a Lord's Day service on Saturday evening for the convenience of worshipers. Other congregations, following the ancient Roman, and modern, practice of counting days from midnight to midnight, hold services Sunday evening. Some Christians find that the whole Lord's Day becomes more meaningful if they worship together both morning and evening.

The Place Where We Meet

Imagine that Sunday has come and that shortly your congregation will be gathering where you customarily worship. We have come early to give ourselves time to look around and reflect. Even if you have seen your church hundreds of time, try to look at it as if you had never seen it before.

The physical space in which a congregation worships has more effect on both the worship and the worshiper than most of us realize. Unless worship is held outdoors, it is held in a room that United Methodists commonly call the *sanctuary*—a term that suggests this room has been designed to help the worshiper be more aware of the sanctity, the sacredness, the holiness of God.

In most churches, particularly medium-sized and larger

ones, there is a hallway or vestibule or lobby, sometimes
called the *narthex,* located between the outer door through
which you enter the building and the inner door through
which you enter the sanctuary. It helps us make the
transition into the spirit of worship by providing a space in
which people may greet and talk with one another, be
welcomed by ushers or greeters or the minister, remove and
hang up wraps, and be reminded by the surroundings that
they are preparing to worship. On cold days it provides a
place to catch your breath after coming in out of the cold
and protects those in the sanctuary from the draft of cold air
when the sanctuary doors are opened. Even in churches
where you step directly into the sanctuary from the
outdoors, there is often a space immediately inside the door
that serves these purposes and is not quite like the rest of the
sanctuary.

Sometimes the sanctuary is reserved strictly for worship,
and sometimes it is used for other purposes during the
week. Sometimes during the hour immediately before or
after Sunday worship this room is used by a Sunday school
assembly or class. Such an arrangement may reflect that the
congregation has limited space, or it may reflect a
preference for an arrangement that makes worship and
study, and perhaps other activities, feel more unified.
Wherever Sunday school is held, many persons feel that it is
part of their preparation for worship. Sometimes persons
who have been in a Sunday school class enter the sanctuary
not through the narthex but directly through some other
door, as if to suggest that they have already had the narthex
experience in Sunday school.

The sanctuary is designed to draw your attention to the
worship center, which is usually on a raised platform and is
the place from which worship is led. This worship center is
likely to contain several key pieces of furniture. The pulpit

is a stand behind or in which the preacher stands to preach and from which other parts of the service may be conducted. Sometimes there is also a lectern, a smaller stand that may be used for reading and the leading of certain other parts of the service. The Lord's table (communion table, altar table) is used for Holy Communion. The baptismal font holds water and is used for baptisms. Somewhere in the sanctuary there are usually seats for the choir or choirs and an organ and/or piano. There are many ways of arranging these basic furnishings, but most United Methodist churches tend to follow one of three basic patterns.

One pattern, sometimes called pulpit-centered, was dominant during the nineteenth and early twentieth centuries and is still common. There is a raised platform with the pulpit in the center. This symbolizes the centrality of the reading and preaching of God's Word. The communion table is usually in front of the pulpit on a lower level. The baptismal font can have various locations, but it is usually to one side on the lower level. The choir may sit in a raised loft behind the pulpit or may sit to one side of the pulpit, but either way choir members face the congregation. There may also be a cross above and behind the pulpit, either hanging or fastened to the wall, to symbolize the presence of God through the risen Christ. The seating is often arranged to bring the people as close as possible to the pulpit and choir. Thus the sanctuary may be wide, there may be no center aisle, the seating may be curved or even semicircular, and there may be a balcony.

A second pattern, sometimes called altar-centered or divided-chancel, was dominant during the middle third of the twentieth century and is still very common. In this pattern there are two distinct worship spaces.

The *chancel,* which is the raised area up front, may be a

large, recessed area behind an archway that is almost a separate room, or it may be simply a platform. Against the center of the far wall is a table, altar, or shelf that is intended to be the center of worship. A cross on or over the altar, lighted candles on or beside the altar, and flowers in the vicinity of the altar all suggest the presence of God through the risen Christ. In this pattern, the term *sanctuary* is applied to the space immediately around the altar rather than to the whole room. The pulpit is on one side of the chancel, and on the other side there is usually a lectern or occasionally a baptismal font. The choir usually sits at right angles to the people, often in two banks on either side of the altar.

The rest of the people sit in the other distinct area, called the *nave*. It is on a level lower than the chancel, and it is likely to be long and narrow, with a center aisle. The people sit in straight rows, all facing the chancel and the altar. Sometimes there are side areas toward the front, called *transepts,* which together with the nave and chancel give the church a cross-shaped floor plan. Seating in the transepts is at right angles to that in the nave, but the people there also face the chancel and altar. In this arrangement the people are encouraged to focus their attention on the altar throughout the service rather than on the preacher or the choir or the congregation.

Often there will be a mixture of patterns in churches built in the first pattern and later modified by renovations in the second pattern.

A third pattern, sometimes called contemporary, has appeared in recent years. A free-standing Lord's table is central but in a more or less equal balance with the pulpit and with the baptismal font. The people are seated so as to be close to these central furnishings and to one another. The room as a whole is unified rather than divided into nave and chancel. The choir may be located in various places, but is obviously intended to be part of the congregation.

Once you have studied the furnishings around which the sanctuary is focused and which are used in the central actions of worship, look at the shell—the walls and floor and ceiling that enclose the sanctuary and define the space. A long, narrow room can suggest the awesome majesty and otherness of God by putting distance between the worshiper and the center of worship, and a square or semicircular or fan-shaped space can bring the people closer to the center of the action and suggest that God is in our midst. Likewise, a high, vaulted ceiling can suggest the majesty of the God who is "high and lifted up"; and a low, flat ceiling can suggest God's nearness. The man who once said to me, "I can't worship under a flat ceiling," was saying something important about what God and worship meant to him, as are the people who tell me they feel closer to God in their little country church than in a great cathedral. Some churches are built in the shape of a large tent in an attempt to suggest both the majesty of God and the presence of God in the midst of a close-knit congregation.

The composition and decoration of the shell of the sanctuary are also important. Carpeting on the floor may seem warmer than hardwood or tile or stone and, together with sound-absorbent ceilings, may also keep down the noise of conversation, but at the high cost of making the singing sound far weaker and forcing more electronic amplification. Banners, flags, and posters may appear on or near the walls. Stained-glass windows are not only symbolic and educational but also let in light of many colors. Have you ever noticed how different your sanctuary looks at various times of the day? The sun may shine through an east window during the morning service and bathe the whole congregation in light, and a west window shows its full glory only in the afternoon. Evening, without sunlight but with electric lights and perhaps candles, make the sanctuary seem quite different. If you have seen your sanctuary only on Sunday mornings, you have missed a great deal.

CHAPTER 2

What's Behind All This?

In the Bible

Now that we have taken a good look at the sanctuary, it's obvious that what goes on there has much history. Suppose that we're still sitting in your church sanctuary and came early to have enough time to think about how our worship came to be as it is today.

Sunday worship services as we know them are rooted in worship as Jesus and his earliest disciples knew it. They were Jews, and their worship was Jewish worship. There were services in the synagogue and family worship that centered around the meal table.

We're not sure just how and when synagogue worship originated, but it may have been in the sixth century B.C. when large numbers of Jews had been taken from their native land and found themselves in exile in Babylon. The Temple in Jerusalem, the center of their worship, had been destroyed. These Jews asked, "How could we sing the Lord's song in a foreign land?" (Psalm 137:4) This may have been when they began to hold gatherings where there were readings from the scriptures (what we call the Old Testament) and interpretations or teaching based on these readings. Interspersed were praises to God, probably including psalms. Such worship could be held anywhere the people could gather and could be led by any man educated well enough in the scriptures to read and interpret them. The term *synagogue,* literally meaning gathering or assembly, was applied first to these assemblies for worship and later also to the buildings built to accommodate these assemblies.

By the time of Jesus and his disciples, the synagogue, along with the home, was where the majority of Jews worshiped each week on the sabbath. The Temple in Jerusalem had been rebuilt, but since most Jews did not live in Jerusalem and could go there only occasionally, if at all, the synagogue where they lived was the center of their community worship.

Jesus began his public ministry by going around his native region of Galilee preaching and teaching in the synagogues. In his hometown of Nazareth, for instance, he went to the synagogue on the sabbath day, as was his custom; read Isaiah 61:1-2 from the scriptures; and then preached to those assembled (Luke 4:16-30).

As Jesus and his disciples traveled together they also ate together, and as devout Jews, they considered these meals sacred occasions to be observed with thanksgiving to God. The family meal table had long been the center of Jewish family worship. Jesus and his disciples, having left their families to travel together, had themselves become a family.

Jesus' supper with his disciples on the night before his death was both the last of these meals and the beginning of a transformed meal that Christians have eaten ever since. That night Jesus added something new to the sacred family meal they had known. As he gave them the bread he said, "This is my body. . . . Do this in remembrance of me" (Matthew 26:26-29; Mark 14:22-25; Luke 22:19-20; 1 Corinthians 11:23-25). When Jesus was killed his disciples were shattered and scattered but two days later on the first Easter they found themselves face-to-face with the living, risen Christ. They found faith and meaning for their lives and a message for the world. Ever since, Christians have been an Easter people.

Luke's Gospel (chapter 24) describes the encounter of the disciples with the living Christ as worship—a transformed synagogue and a transformed holy meal. When two disciples walking from Jerusalem to Emmaus had been joined by Jesus and had poured out their hearts to him, he quoted to them extensively from Moses and all the prophets (parts of what Christians call the Old Testament) and "interpreted" these scriptures to them—a term that to Luke's readers would clearly mean what was done in the synagogue. When they got to Emmaus and sat down to their evening meal, Jesus began to do what he had done before at such meals; and he was "known to them in the breaking of the bread." Later that evening in Jerusalem, he appeared to a larger group of disciples, ate in their presence, and "opened their minds to understand the scriptures."

John's Gospel (chapters 20–21) not only tells of the risen Christ's eating breakfast with his disciples but also tells how Thomas, when he encountered the risen Christ, said, "My Lord and my God!" Ever since, Christians have experienced encounters with the risen Christ as encounters with God.

We read that Jesus then ascended into heaven, is at the right hand of God, and "fills all in all" (Acts 1:9-11; Ephesians 1:20-23). He promised his disciples, "I am with you always" (Matthew 28:20). In other words, just as God is everywhere and can be encountered and worshiped anywhere, so can the risen and ascended Christ.

Furthermore, Jesus promised at his ascension, "You will receive power when the Holy Spirit has come upon you;" and this happened on the day of Pentecost (Acts 1–2). From that day to this, Christian worship has been an encounter with the living God through the risen Christ in the power of the Holy Spirit. This is one way of defining Christian worship.

After the disciples went out preaching and teaching with the power of the Spirit on the day of Pentecost, sometimes called the birthday of the Christian church, they continued to take part in synagogue worship wherever they went (Acts 9:2, 20; 13:5, 14ff; 14:1; 17:1ff, 10ff; 18:4, 19, 26; 19:8; 22:19; 24:12; 26:11) and to break bread as a holy meal in their own gatherings (Acts 2:42, 46). Their preaching and teaching about Christ in the synagogues eventually led to a break between the Christian church and Jewish synagogues, and the Christians held their own adaptation of the synagogue service when they gathered on the first day of the week for "the breaking of bread." Such a combined service is described in Acts 20:7-12. Interspersed with reading and preaching the Word of God, these Christians would "sing psalms, hymns, and spiritual songs to God" (Colossians 3:16).

Through the Centuries

About A.D. 155 Justin Martyr, writing in his *First Apology* to pagans to correct vicious rumors about what Christians did when they gathered for worship, gave this description of Christian Sunday worship:

> The memoirs of the apostles [that later became the New Testament] or the writings of the prophets [Old Testament] are read as long as time permits. When the reader has finished, the presider in a discourse [sermon] urges and invites [us] to the imitation of these noble things. Then we all stand up and offer prayers. . . . When we have finished the prayer, bread is brought, and wine with water, and the presider similarly sends up prayers and thanksgivings to the best of his ability, and the congregation assents, saying the

> Amen; the distribution and reception of the consecrated
> [bread and wine] by each one takes place and they are sent to
> the absent by deacons. (Chapter 67)

Because these Christians were under persecution and had
to meet secretly in homes, it is likely that services were held
quietly and in haste and that anything noisy or nonessential
was omitted. This may account for the omission of any
reference to singing psalms, hymns, and spiritual songs—
which would probably have been sung when possible. This
may also account for the fact that the holy meal, originally a
full meal, had been reduced to bread and wine, although
this change may also have been a reaction to abuses such as
the overeating and overdrinking by some while others went
hungry, as described in 1 Corinthians 11:17-22.

Christianity grew, and by the fourth century it ceased to
be persecuted and became the official religion of the Roman
Empire. Christians could now worship openly, build
elaborate church buildings, and expand their worship
services to include ceremonial entrances and glorious acts of
prayer and praise. Yet Sunday worship retained at its core
the synagogue service in Christian form, followed by the
holy meal—what we call the Service of Word and Table.

Gradually, however, other things began to obscure the
essentials and abuses crept in. In western Europe, Latin
continued to be the language of worship after it had ceased
to be the language of the people. Preaching declined and
often disappeared, although from time to time there were
outstanding efforts to renew it. There was still the Holy
Communion, but it became something done by the
presiding priest, in buildings that made the area where the
clergy functioned (the chancel) increasingly separate and
far removed from where the people were gathered (the
nave). Fewer and fewer people came forward to receive

communion, and a church law had to be enacted requiring Christians to receive communion at least once a year. By the fourteenth century, only priests were permitted to drink from the cup; laypersons could eat only the bread, which had become a wafer rather than real bread.

The Protestant Reformation in the sixteenth century attempted to reform these abuses, but its success was only partial. The Roman Catholic Church rejected the Protestant reforms and retained the allegiance of most Christians in western Europe. The Eastern Orthodox Church and the ancient oriental churches, which had long since become separated from the Roman Catholic Church, were untouched. The Protestant churches under the leadership of Martin Luther, John Calvin, and others were successful in restoring the reading and preaching of the scriptures in the language of the people and in restoring congregational singing of Psalms and other forms of song. Some Protestants also restored the freedom to pray extemporaneously rather than being limited to set prayer texts.

Less successful were the attempts by the Reformation leaders to restore the fullness of Holy Communion. They did restore the right of laypersons to drink from the cup as well as eat the bread. They also restored the practice that those present at Holy Communion would partake unless there was some reason why they should not. The words used were translated into the language of the people, and there were earnest attempts to come to a more biblical understanding of the meaning of Holy Communion.

On the other hand, Holy Communion came to be celebrated only occasionally—usually quarterly or monthly—because the people, conditioned by centuries of rarely receiving communion, rebelled at receiving it more often. Luther and Calvin believed that Holy Communion was the natural and appropriate act to follow the weekly Service of the Word, and Calvin left record of his deep disappointment at his inability to persuade the people at this point. They were also unable to restore to Holy Communion its original spirit of joyful celebration. It tended to be penitential and even funereal.

During the next two centuries we see a mixed picture of renewal and deterioration of worship. Strong attempts were made to insist that at least two readings (often two complete chapters) of scripture be read and that the sermon be interpretations of scripture. Much congregational song was written and sung, including Psalm settings. In both Catholic and Protestant churches there was more elaborate choral and instrumental praise. Some Protestant churches managed to celebrate Holy Communion every Sunday, although popular resistance to taking communion that often eventually caused this practice largely to die out.

There were a number of strong renewal movements in the eighteenth century in Europe and in the eighteenth and early nineteenth centuries in America, and The United Methodist Church is directly descended from three of these movements. In England, John Wesley (1703–1791), a priest of the Church of England, founded Methodism. His brother Charles (1707–1788) wrote many popular hymns and set them to familiar tunes that the people could readily learn. Francis Asbury (1745–1816) led Wesley's followers in establishing American Methodism. Also in America, Jacob Albright (1759–1808) founded the Evangelical branch of the Evangelical United Brethren Church; and Philip Otterbein (1726–1813) and Martin Boehm (1725–1812) founded the United Brethren. They all emphasized scriptural preaching to those who were not being reached by the churches at that time. The Wesleys also believed in Holy Communion as one of the key means of grace and tried, unsuccessfully, to restore its celebration each Sunday.

In Modern America

Since the eighteenth century, worship in the denominations that have now united to form The United Methodist Church has gone through several phases.

During the first of these, from the late eighteenth century until the early twentieth century, the central concern was evangelism or church growth. When our nation won its independence, less than 10 percent of the population belonged to any church, but by the mid-twentieth century over 60 percent of the people were affiliated with some religious denomination. From their beginnings in the late eighteenth century the predecessor denominations of The United Methodist Church grew, and by 1850 they included three out of every eight American church members. In the late nineteenth and early twentieth centuries they continued to grow, but they maintained a steadily decreasing proportion of American church members.

At first, and in the most successful days of church growth, there was a strong emphasis on biblical preaching; but as growth slowed and preachers tried harder to give their sermons popular appeal, preaching became less biblical. Methodist preachers in the early nineteenth century were officially instructed to read a chapter from the Old Testament and a chapter from the New Testament before they preached. By the latter part of the century this had changed to a *reading* from the Old Testament and a reading from the New Testament. In the early twentieth century provision was made that a responsive reading from the Psalms could be substituted for the Old Testament reading, and later orders of worship mentioned simply a single scripture reading and a responsive reading. Often even these were omitted.

At first preaching tended to be based on a passage of

scripture, then on a single verse of scripture. This text often became a pretext for a sermon that did not interpret the meaning of the text at all but instead used a key word or phrase or image to launch into an unrelated topic that appealed to the preacher. Then in the early twentieth century it became fashionable to begin a sermon with a life situation or illustration rather than reading or quoting a text. Sometimes a text was introduced in the middle of the sermon, but sometimes it disappeared entirely.

Congregational song, meanwhile, developed from the singing of Psalms, to the singing of hymns and songs that were saturated with biblical imagery and thought, to the singing of hymns and songs that made little or no reference to scripture.

The second phase was the "high church" or aesthetic or romantic movement that developed in England in the nineteenth century and became increasingly popular in American Protestant churches in the early and middle twentieth century. As church people became more sophisticated, they became more demanding in their aesthetic taste. For many churches, the desire to retain their members became dominant over the desire to grow. Many thought that by making services impressive—even awesome—in their beauty, people who had outgrown simpler expressions of religion would continue to find worship meaningful. There was a concern to enrich worship, to restore old traditions (though these were usually from the Middle Ages rather than the early church), and to offer to God the most beautiful music and liturgies and art.

The service itself was commonly divided into two parts. The first part of the service was an increasingly elaborate and formal "morning worship," which included printed unison and responsive prayers and other acts of worship as well as anthems and responses by the choir. Scripture was usually read, but with little or no expectation that it was to be the basis for the preaching. In the middle of the service was a sort of intermission, consisting typically of announcements, offering, and hymn. The sermon constituted the latter part of the service. It was prefaced by little or no reading of scripture and had little or no connection with the first part of the service.

This movement romanticized the Middle Ages as the Age of Faith and the great medieval cathedrals as supreme expressions of faith. Protestant churches were designed to look medieval. If that was too expensive, churches adopted as much of the altar-centered, divided-chancel pattern as they could.

A third phase, sometimes called the contemporary or experimental worship movement, was widely fashionable in the 1960s and 1970s. Here the ideal was not the great cathedral but a small group of people seated in a circle surrounded by banners and posters and other artifacts made by the people themselves. Traditional forms and patterns were looked on with suspicion, and variety was valued for its own sake. Readings may have been from contemporary sources as well as from scripture. Songs may have been anything current (religious or secular) that reflected the people's feelings or the world they lived in. Preaching tended to be a commentary on current events or trends or a best-selling book. There were constant attempts to find new symbolic actions such as sending up balloons or forming the congregation into a snake dance to make worship, in a key phrase of the movement, "the celebration of life." There was little interest in building new sanctuaries; existing sanctuaries were adapted or multipurpose rooms were used for this kind of worship.

These movements have all peaked and declined,

although many congregations are still caught up in them and the influence of these movements is still very much with us.

Today the trend is back to basics, back to our roots, back to the Bible. We are indebted to the scholars who over the years have rediscovered the origins of Christian worship in the Bible and the early church and who have made it possible for us to recover our heritage more authentically than was possible for the church in earlier reforms. We are also indebted to the countless people in our churches who have seen or sensed over the years that we were drifting away from the Bible and from our heritage and who tried to warn those who would listen. We are discovering that in many ways the church today has more in common with the early church than with the established Christendom of the centuries in between.

United Methodists, together with other Christians today, are working to recover both the Service of the Word and Holy Communion, and to find a balance and interrelationship between the two that strengthens both. We have been realizing how we let the Service of the Word deteriorate and how we have neglected Holy Communion. Resources such as *The United Methodist Hymnal* have been designed to help us recover our heritage. There is a searching for contemporary sanctuary designs that express and support this renewed worship.

As you follow the order of worship in your local church, you are likely to see evidence of some or all of these phases of our worship history. Your congregation may be working to renew its worship, and there may be controversy about what is being done. After this chapter on history, it is appropriate to ask what worship is and what guidelines there are by which we can evaluate it.

CHAPTER 3

What's Happening Here?

An Encounter with the Risen Christ

Suppose we are still in the sanctuary of your church waiting for the service to begin and have time to think about what is—or should be—happening when we worship.

We have seen that in the New Testament worship was an encounter with the living God through the risen Christ in the power of the Holy Spirit. Today we are in the midst of a movement of Christians to reclaim our biblical heritage and recover this kind of worship. Is there a particular story in the Bible that can help us see what Christian worship can be?

I believe that the encounter of the disciples with the risen Christ described in Luke 24:13-35 is just such a story.

As on the first day of the week the two disciples were walking together on the road to Emmaus and were joined by the risen Christ, so we come together as a congregation and are joined by the risen and ascended Christ in the power of the Holy Spirit.

As the risen Christ encouraged those disciples to pour out their hearts to him, so he does with us. As those disciples poured out their disillusionment and sadness, so may we if that is our condition. As the disciples later that evening poured out their faith and joy when they gathered in Jerusalem and again met the risen Christ (Luke 24:33-49), so may we in our opening acts of greeting and praise. In any case, just as those disciples needed to open up and share what was in their hearts before they were able to hear Jesus interpret God's Word to them, so by opening our hearts we become ready to hear God's Word.

As Jesus opened the scriptures to those first disciples and their hearts burned within them, so we hear the scriptures opened to us today and out of the burning of our hearts praise God.

As those disciples came to a point where a response was called for, so do we. They did not say good-bye to Jesus but invited him to stay with them, and we can do the same.

As those disciples and the risen Christ came together around the table, so can we. As Jesus did the same four actions—taking, blessing, breaking, and giving—with the bread that the disciples had seen him do just three days before at the Last Supper, as we shall see later, we, too, do these actions with the bread and cup. As "he was known to them in the breaking of the bread," so the risen Christ can be known to us in Holy Communion.

As the risen Christ disappeared and sent the disciples forth into the world with faith and joy, so the risen Christ sends us forth into the world. And as those disciples found Christ when they arrived at Jerusalem, we can find that he is with us wherever we go.

The Drama of Life

Comparing the week-by-week worship of your local church with the Easter story may sound impossibly idealistic. The gap may seem too great to be bridged. How do I get from worship as I have known it to worship as it should be, especially if I am not in control of the worship in my church and I am just sitting in a pew?

Maybe part of our problem is that many of us see worship as if it were a performance in which the preacher and choir are actors and a chorus on stage and we are the audience, watching and listening, ready to criticize the performance after it is complete. We hear the preacher talk *about* God and Jesus, but it may never occur to us that God through Christ is present and taking part in what is going on.

If we think of worship as a drama, it is a far greater drama than that, as Søren Kierkegaard told us over a century ago *(Purity of Heart,* Part XII). The stage is not just the chancel or platform, it is the whole sanctuary, and the entire congregation are actors. The pastor is both the director and one of the actors. God is both the audience and the playwright. The script is the scriptures, and the play is the drama of life.

We can think of worship as the rehearsal of life. Like other rehearsals, worship services should not be too cut-and-dried if learning is to occur. The pastor, as director, has studied the script, interprets it, adapts to the situation in which the drama is taking place (life here and now), and works to bring the actors and the action together into a coherent whole. But remember, the Playwright is present and has the right to interpret the script. The Playwright doesn't have to sit back passively beyond the footlights; but may walk on stage and mingle with the actors. The Playwright may whisper to the director, who in turn can relay the word to the other actors, but is equally free to speak directly to any of the actors. After a service the actors scatter, better prepared to perform their various roles in the drama of life all through the week.

But worship services are more than rehearsals; they are life itself as it should be lived. They do not take place simply for the sake of what happens during the rest of the week; they are the crucial part of the performance that serves as model for all the rest. When we are gathered together in our services of worship, we relate as Christians to God and to other people, and when we are scattered in the world, we are to do the same.

What would happen to you if you took this understanding seriously? What would happen to your congregation if even a few persons dared to take it seriously? Do you dare to believe that your life is part of a vast drama and that your part is important in the eyes of the Playwright, even though you may not know the whole plot and even though your local congregation may be a tiny fraction of the entire cast? Are you studying the script at home and listening attentively as it is interpreted by the director? Are you sensitive to the other actors, relating your role to theirs and learning from them? Are you alert to hear whatever the Playwright may be saying to you? Are you learning so that in the coming week you will play your part well in the drama of life?

Worship Is Central

Such an understanding makes it clear that worship is central to the church as a whole, to your local church, and to your participation as a Christian in the church and the world.

In worship we discover that we *are* the church. We are reminded of who we are and what, by God's grace, we are becoming. As important as it is to ask and plan what your local church is *doing* as the church, the most basic thing is *being* the church. You can leave out any other part of the program of your local church, as important as it may be, and still have a church if you have regular worship. But if you don't have congregational worship you don't have a church.

The living Christ who promised, "I am with you always,"

does for the congregation at worship, week after week, what he did for those scattered disciples on the first Easter day—but with this difference: now, in the power of the Holy Spirit, we can come joyfully *expecting* an encounter with the risen Christ and focusing our attention on the fact of his presence. He bonds us to himself and to one another anew as his people, his family, his Body. He enables the Body to grow, gives to each member of the Body the gifts needed in the role to which he calls that person, and empowers the church corporately for its witness in the world.

It is no wonder that in most local churches more people are present for Sunday worship than at any other time and for any other purpose during the week. Even if there are other occasions when as many people attend as on Sunday morning—an evangelistic service, a church school assembly, some other special service—these are almost always worship services, or at least occasions when worship is an important part of what takes place.

Often in worldwide church history congregations have flourished with only one scheduled activity each week— Sunday worship—during which children, youth, and adults of every age were trained and educated, counseled and advised, nurtured and supported, and equipped for what they were to do during the week. Today many churches of small membership have an effective ministry with no regular weekly meetings except congregational worship and perhaps a Sunday school that includes worship.

Imagine the church forced to cut back its program to the absolute minimum, as in times of persecution. There have been, and still are, times and places where congregations as we think of them have not been permitted, where they could gather only as families and small groups in secret. When they managed to come together in such circumstances, their chief and often their only, corporate activity was worship.

Even in a large congregation with an extensive daily program, corporate worship is central. To be sure, its members often feel more of a sense of belonging to a Sunday school class, an organization, or a small group within the congregation than to the congregation as a whole. But these smaller groups are likely to have times of worship in their meetings; and the main congregational services of worship are the central act by which a large and diverse congregation is, and feels itself to be, one congregation rather than many.

It is in congregational worship, therefore, that a local church is most open to change and growth. Nothing will permeate the whole life of a congregation with the felt presence and power of God as deeply and extensively as the coming to life of its worship. While spiritual renewal can originate in a local church elsewhere than in its congregational worship, that renewal will either bring new life to the congregational worship or be severely limited, if not stifled, by the continuing deadness of that worship.

Worship is crucial in winning persons to Christ and his church. When persons first visit your local church, they probably come with questions that make their first impression of your worship crucial to their whole future relationship with your church and perhaps to their Christian faith. As they take part in the worship of your church, they will be forming impressions that help them answer their questions. Is this the kind of church I am looking for? What does it stand for? Is there anything here that meets my needs? Are these people who I would like to be associated with? Could I become enthusiastic about what this church is doing? If they decide to join your church, what they have experienced in worship will probably have been an important part of the reason.

As Christians, we need to be part of a supportive worshiping community if we are to be nurtured and grow in the faith. Even if we are familiar with the gospel message, we need to be reminded of it regularly. We need a deeper understanding of the story and teachings of the Bible. We need to participate in public prayer and learn from the example of other Christians how to pray and praise God in any setting, public or private. We need a model of how Christians show love to one another and act out the gospel. We need to broaden our horizons by meeting members of the Body of Christ with differing gifts and perspectives and to become, in the process, better grounded and more mature Christians.

Basic Principles of Worship

This whole understanding of worship suggests certain basic principles that can help us know what to want and what to look for in worship.

1. *God's Word is primary.* It is given to us in scripture, which is the "script" on which our worship is based and our primary source for discerning what is of God. It is opened to the people by the reading of scripture and its faithful interpretation through preaching. Over a period of time this should include a full and balanced coverage of the entire Bible. Prayer and praise gain added power when they use words of scripture.

2. *Active congregational participation is crucial.* The responses of the people to God's Word are necessary if worship is to be a two-way sharing process. Prayer and praise, therefore, play a major role in worship. The people should be enabled to share the full range of their joys and sorrows, their needs and concerns. God has given to

members of any congregation varieties of gifts; and the particular gifts of laypersons as well as clergy are needed, not only in acts of worship but also in its planning, leadership, and evaluation.

3. *Spontaneity and order are both important.* Worship should be open to both the planned and the unexpected movings of the Spirit, who can speak not only through the preacher but through anyone present. Persons feel free to follow the Spirit if they have a basic sense of pattern and structure, within which there is freedom and from which one may occasionally depart. Both rigidity on the one hand and chaos on the other make most people withdraw into their shells.

4. *Worship should be relevant and inclusive.* Because God relates to all of life, so should worship. It should relate to and include the people's memories, experiences, needs, and hopes. It should include the stranger as well as those already part of the congregation. It should include emotion as well as thought, the body as well as the mind, and each one of the senses. It should include children, youth, and adults of all ages in such a way that persons of every level of spiritual development can be reached by God's Word and appropriately respond. It should include men and women of every ethnic and cultural heritage to which the congregation has access, as well as persons with handicapping conditions. All these persons should be enabled to offer their gifts as well as their needs in worship.

5. *Worship is communion.* It is communion between God and the gathered congregation and communion of persons with God and with one another. It moves through call-and-response sharing to climactic times when we have a foretaste of the heavenly banquet and know ourselves to be "one with Christ, one with each other, and one in ministry

to all the world." While the Spirit can give this gift when we least expect it, Christ gives us a regular opportunity for such a foretaste in Holy Communion. This sacrament should have the major role in congregational worship that it had in New Testament worship.

The Order of Worship

We saw in chapter 2 that there is a historic order to the Service of Word and Table, but that this order has been subject to wide variation.

What sort of order does Sunday worship have in your church? When you walk into the worship service in your church, you are probably given a leaflet containing the printed order of the service that day. This is often called the bulletin. Whether or not there is a bulletin, there is usually a pattern to the service that is familiar to those who attend regularly. Within that pattern there may be flexibility, and on special occasions the usual pattern may not be followed at all. Most of the time, however, the regular worshiper has a good idea what will come next, even without looking at a bulletin. A church may go through a stage in its history when it is ready for a trusted pastor or other leaders to take it through a period of experimentation, but even then it usually is not long before a pattern emerges.

The United Methodist Church has a book to help congregations worship. As you sit in your church, you will probably find a copy of *The United Methodist Hymnal* in the hymnal rack. Notice that on its title page it is subtitled *Book of United Methodist Worship,* because it is our book of congregational worship.

Look at the table of contents. You will notice that the first fifty-four pages contain the General Services that are used in weekly congregational worship. These come first because they are the framework within which the Hymns, Canticles & Acts of Worship that follow take their place. Next is the Psalter—the psalms in a format suitable for worship. Then come the Other General Services that take place at some time other than weekly congregational worship. Then comes a collection of Acts of Worship near the back of the book for easy reference during worship. Finally there are several indexes.

Turn to page 2 of the hymnal and examine The Basic Pattern of Worship. You will notice that it is not an item-by-item order of worship such as you probably find in your local church bulletin, but a more general pattern to guide both those who plan worship and all of us who seek to understand it. You will notice that it is based on Luke 24:13-35. It is a pattern that allows for a great deal of variety, and you will probably see that the order of worship in your local church bulletin on a typical Sunday is based on it.

On pages 3-5 you will find An Order of Sunday Worship Using the Basic Pattern. While no order of worship can be flexible enough to show all the diversity that exists in The United Methodist Church, this order shows some of the variety that is possible within the basic pattern. These pages, like the basic pattern, are not intended for the congregation to follow during a worship service but are a resource for those who plan or seek to understand United Methodist worship. You may wish to compare this order with the order in your local church bulletin. If your local order of worship is distinctively different, you might try to learn about its history and why it was developed.

You may also find a Bible in the hymnal rack. This enables worshipers to follow scripture readings during the service with their eyes as well as their ears. Some congregations also use pew Bibles for reading scripture in unison.

So far we have imagined that we were sitting quietly in your church sanctuary, observing everything in our surroundings that help us worship, and reflecting on how Christian worship came to be and what makes it authentically and effectively Christian. Now the service begins.

CHAPTER 4

The Service Begins

When Does the Service Begin?

People are beginning to gather in the sanctuary. Actually, the gathering begins, not in the sanctuary, but in the parking lot, on the way into the building, outside the sanctuary, as people begin to encounter one another. Some are members of the congregation who begin to renew their sense of being part of the community of faith the moment they meet others on the way toward the sanctuary. There are also strangers, who from the moment they drive into the parking lot are experiencing welcome and Christian community—or the lack of it. The pastor and choir are not yet in place, and no music is being played. We might wonder, "When does the service begin?"

We saw in chapter 2 that from early Christian times worship services have been called "gatherings." The word *congregation* is derived from a verb meaning "to flock together." The translated New Testament word *church* means "assembly" or "gathering." Many Christians refer to worship as "meeting" or "having church." If we take this understanding seriously, then the service begins whenever people start to gather for worship.

The Gathering

We use the term "Gathering" to refer specifically to the first part of the service when the people are literally in the process of gathering. During the Gathering, one or more of the following may take place:

1. A church bell or bells or amplified music may sound from the church tower through the neighborhood to call people to worship.

2. As the people come together there may be informal greetings, conversation, and fellowship. This renewing of community is an important part of our entrance into congregational worship. It is essential that strangers receive a warm welcome if they are to feel part of the worshiping congregations.

3. There may be informal singing.

4. After the congregation has fully gathered, there may be the public welcoming or introduction of visitors (which may take the form of a Ritual of Friendship, using pads or cards that people sign), announcements, or rehearsal of unfamiliar hymns or other congregational acts of worship. (These acts may also take place at a later point in the service.)

5. Organ or other instrumental music may be played in the sanctuary to encourage quiet meditation, reflection, or prayer. There may also be opportunity for prayer in a separate prayer room or chapel. Worship leaders and choirs commonly pray together before entering the sanctuary.

6. Candles may be lit by persons called *acolytes*.

7. If there is no processional hymn, the worship leaders and choir(s) may enter and take their places.

These customs may be combined in various ways. None of these combinations in itself is better or worse than the others, but in a particular local church or on a particular occasion one may be more appropriate than another.

More than meets the eye is happening while the people gather. God is present through the risen Christ in the power of the Holy Spirit. Present in spirit, too, is the Body of

Christ. We who gather here today are not simply fifty, or five hundred, members of one local church who live in the same community and are affiliated with the same denomination. We are "a great multitude that no one could count, from every nation, from all tribes and peoples and languages, standing before the throne and before the Lamb, robed in white . . . saying, 'Salvation belongs to our God, who is seated on the throne, and to the Lamb [Christ]!' " (Revelation 7:9-10). If the seating arrangement in your sanctuary is slightly curved, as if a segment of a much larger circle of seating going around your pulpit and table, it may suggest to you that the few people visibly present in your sanctuary today are only a small part of a much larger circle, the family of Christ, which neither distance nor denominational barriers nor death can break. Our gathering includes the whole communion of saints— those who have died, those who live in the world today, and generations yet unborn who will praise God's name.

There are special moments when the leaders of worship enter the gathering. The organist or other instrumentalists may be the first of these to enter. The pastor may be present throughout the gathering, informally greeting people, or may quietly enter at some point during the gathering, or may enter as part of a procession. The choir(s), too, may enter quietly or as a singing procession. There may be other persons such as one or more associate pastors, a song leader, or one or more laypersons assisting in the leadership of the service. One or two acolytes may enter and light candles either at some point during the gathering or as part of a procession.

Some or all of these persons may be wearing robes or vestments. An academic robe, sometimes worn with a hood, signifies the educational preparation and teaching ministry of the pastor. An alb, a white or light-colored robe adapted from the basic garment worn by men and women alike in the early days of Christianity, is a link with the early Christians and symbolizes the presence of the whole communion of saints—the "great multitude . . . robed in white." Albs may be properly worn by laypersons as well as by ordained ministers. On the other hand, the stole (colored scarf) worn around the neck and hanging down in front over an alb or academic robe, has from ancient times signified that the wearer is ordained.

A Variety of Gifts

As we look at these worship leaders, let's consider their roles. Paul tells us (1 Corinthians 12) that there are varieties of gifts and varieties of service in the Body of Christ.

Let's start with those persons, whether ordained ministers or laypersons, who lead worship. They are sometimes spokespersons for God to the people, as when reading scripture and preaching, and sometimes spokespersons for the people to God, as when leading prayer. Today more and more laypersons are assuming such leadership roles in worship. This is following ancient Christian custom and has brought new life to many congregations.

What distinctive gifts, then, does the ordained minister bring to worship and what does ordination authorize a minister to do in worship? Ordination authorizes the minister (1) to preach the Word (interpret the scriptures); (2) to officiate at baptisms, Holy Communion, weddings, and funerals; and (3) to order the worship of the congregation within the prescribed guidelines. In some United Methodist congregations where no ordained minister is available, the bishop may give an unordained pastor temporary and local authorization to carry on these essential ministries.

The ordained minister is the authorized representative of the wider church and its heritage in the local congregation at worship, so that this worship may be more fully the worship of the whole communion of saints. The wider church certifies by ordination its belief that this minister (1) has been called by God to this particular ministry; (2) has the faith, commitment, and gifts required for this ministry; and (3) has undergone the studies and other preparation necessary for this ministry. The church, through a process involving both the congregations out of which candidates come and then the wider denomination (district and annual conference), examines candidates for ordination, certifies that they are called and qualified, and then ordains them with the invocation of the Holy Spirit.

Choir directors, choir members, and those who play musical instruments bring special gifts to worship through the ministry of music—their calling and commitment, their talents, their training and education, and their experience. This is true of the ready and willing persons with little or no training who offer the best that they have to give, just as it is true of the professional musicians who offer their best.

Actually, the whole congregation acts as the choir in the singing of hymns, songs, choruses, and responses, and acts as a speaking choir in unison prayer and other unison and responsive acts of worship. This is part of what was meant by the statement that the whole congregation are actors in worship. The congregation, however, usually includes one or more smaller ensembles (choirs) and instrumentalists to strengthen the worship of the congregation in three basic ways:

1. They can lead the rest of the congregation in worship. They can strengthen and enliven congregational singing, particularly if a congregation is learning something new. If they are seated where the rest of the congregation can see

them, they can cue the others when to stand and sit and can use their body language to be an effective example of attentive worship.

2. They can be spokespersons for the whole congregation to God. Some acts of worship—anthems, for instance—require rehearsal for which the congregation as a whole cannot be expected to give time, and often demand special abilities and training that most of the congregation do not have. Listeners can identify with such acts of worship and feel that the choir and instrumentalists are being their spokespersons—offering an act of worship on their behalf—to God. Much music today helps congregations do this by including parts for the congregation as well as for the soloists or choir.

3. They can be spokespersons for God to the congregation. God speaks powerfully to people through music. Scriptures are often opened and Christian witness given, most effectively when set to music of a type that must be sung or played by an individual or by a small group rather than by the whole congregation.

There are also special gifts brought to worship by ushers and greeters. Their leadership is especially important in the Gathering, at the offering, and during Holy Communion.

Other special gifts are brought by those who provide or arrange flowers, altar cloths, banners, and other visuals. And sometimes worship is enriched by gifts of drama, sacred dance, and related arts.

We remember the custodian or whoever cleans and prepares the sanctuary for services, the secretary or whoever produces the bulletin, the acolytes and those who train them, and all the other persons in the church who have some assigned role in services.

When we add to all these gifts those that come from rank-and-file members of the congregation, and when we remember all the past leadership that still influences what a congregation expects when at worship, we have a wide diversity that is rewarding and perhaps sometimes hard to live with. We may think of each pastor or musician who comes along, "Why isn't he or she like so-and-so?" and wonder why we're always disappointed; or we can ask, "What gifts does this person have for us?" and help him or her to grow in the exercise of these gifts. The fussy baby, those who are moved to praise the Lord in the most unexpected time and way, the critic who mumbles a complaining commentary on the service, and the monotone who makes more noise than a dozen people singing in tune are in the same service with the perfectionists who feel that their worship has been spoiled if the slightest thing goes wrong, the short-fused who shoot a glare or a frown in the direction of anyone who is the slightest bit conspicuous, and the children of any age looking for the slightest excuse to chuckle or snicker. There is no way you or I can make the rest of the congregation behave the way we wish, but if we add our gifts to theirs we can all be enriched by what has taken place.

CHAPTER 5

Prayer and Praise

The Greetings

The first major turning point in the worship service occurs when the pastor, choir, or other leaders of worship begin speaking or singing in such a manner as to draw the whole congregation into a call-and-response sequence in which the people are in audible dialogue with God and with one another in God's name. The pastor or some other leader may greet the people in the Lord's name and call them to worship God, and the people may respond by greeting God with a hymn of praise. Sometimes the first words are a hymn of praise to God, during which the choir, pastor, and other worship leaders may enter in a procession and after which a leader (not necessarily the pastor) greets the people in the Lord's name and calls them to some further response such as prayer. Sometimes the choir sings a call (or *introit*), which leads to a response in which the people greet God with praise or prayer. A leader may begin by invoking the Trinity or by reading or quoting a sentence of scripture in which God is calling to the people, and the people respond with praise or prayer to God.

These patterns are all greetings—both people-to-people in the Lord's name and also between the gathered people and God. As such, they all involve call and response. An understanding of call-and-response patterns is basic to an understanding of our worship.

Worship is a dialogue, a conversation, a sharing, an exchange, a communion between God and the gathered congregation and also among God's gathered people. It is a very special kind of dialogue, as these opening greetings illustrate. A leader or choir greets the people not simply as one person to another, but in the Lord's name—that is, in the name of God and of the risen Christ. We acknowledge that God has initiated the dialogue and is acting through whoever is speaking or singing the greeting. The people respond not simply to the person or persons who address them but to God.

This dialogue is carried on with more than words and music. We have already seen that in churches the worshipers are surrounded with visual symbolism—messages for your eyes. The physical sensation of standing or kneeling or bowing our heads helps us be more alert and sensitive to God's communications to us as well as more expressive in our prayer and praise to God. As we continue to study our worship, we shall discover that all our senses are channels of communion with God and with one another in worship.

As we become more aware that we are in dialogue with God, we can be more alert to promptings that come to us through no outward senses but are channels of God's presence and guidance. The God who is closer than our breathing is nearer than we think.

Acts of Prayer and Praise

After the opening greetings typically there are acts of congregational prayer and praise. These may be simply an opening hymn of praise and a prayer, followed perhaps by an anthem. This part of the service may be expanded into a more elaborate sequence of formal praises and prayers or of informal singing.

There are likely to be prayers and praises later in the service as well, as the order of Sunday worship on pages 3-5 of our hymnal indicates.

Whatever the pattern in your local church, let's take a look at what happens in congregational prayer and praise.

Prayer is a response to God's call and is part of an ongoing call-and-response pattern that characterizes all our worship. The call, given in the Lord's name, may be simply, "Let us pray." It may be a longer sentence, or an exchange between leader and people, or a call to prayer by the choir.

Prayers in response to such calls may be led by a single person or by several persons in turn, or it may alternate between leader and people (a form sometimes called a *litany)*, or it may be prayed in unison by the congregation or by a choir. Persons leading the prayer are praying on behalf of the whole congregation, and indeed we are being joined in prayer by the whole communion of saints. Sometimes a prayer is an alternation of calls and prayers, sometimes called a *bidding prayer*. All these prayers may be spoken, or they may be sung. A large proportion of our hymns, choruses, and anthems are prayers. A choir or soloist singing a prayer is leading the congregation in prayer just as much as is a pastor praying a pastoral prayer.

When the congregation is led in prayer, it is traditional for the people to affirm the prayer by responding "amen"—which in Hebrew means "so be it" or "I agree." When the people say or sing "amen" at the end of a prayer, it means that they agree with the prayer and are making it their own. It is much more appropriate that this "amen" be said or sung by the whole congregation rather than by the leader or choir alone.

Even if your congregation is not used to saying this "amen" out loud, you can quietly say it yourself. More and more persons have been doing this in recent years, and in many congregations this practice has caught on until "amens" are heard all over the congregation and finally acknowledged as something the congregation does.

In many congregations the people say "amen" or "yes, Lord" or "praise the Lord" or similar words at any point in a prayer when they feel moved to do so. Sometimes this is done very quietly, especially if there is reason to fear that other worshipers may not appreciate such interjections. In other congregations it is accepted and done aloud.

A congregation can pray by means other than speech. We can pray silently, and times of silent prayer are part of many worship services. Through interpretive movement or sacred dance, one person or a few persons or a whole congregation may pray in body language, either in silence or while words of prayer are being spoken or sung. Congregations of the deaf worship in sign language. In many other congregations someone signs what is said or sung—that is, interprets it in sign language—not only for those who cannot hear the words but also because many persons who can hear the words find that signing adds another dimension to their prayer.

In any public prayer the congregation expresses its participation by some form of body language. In biblical times and in the ancient church people stood for prayer, and congregations often do today. (See 1 Samuel 1:26; Matthew 6:5; Mark 11:25; Luke 18:11.) Sometimes the leader, and perhaps other persons as well, adds the biblical raising of somewhat outstretched hands, especially if the prayer is one of praise or thanksgiving. (See 1 Kings 8:22; Psalms 28:2, 63:4, 134:2, 141:2; Isaiah 1:15; Lamentations 2:19, 3:41; 1 Timothy 2:8.) Other persons and congregations kneel, especially if the prayer is one of confession. Still others remain seated, perhaps bowing their heads and sitting straight and alert. Some persons pray most naturally with their eyes closed, others with their eyes open. One posture is not necessarily correct and the others wrong; persons and congregations are free to decide what posture is most appropriate as they pray to God.

There are different kinds of prayer. *Praise* is adoration and thanksgiving for God's own goodness and power. It overlaps with *thanksgiving,* which may be praise or may be giving thanks for the gifts God has given us. *Petition* or *supplication* is asking God to act on our behalf. Two special forms of petition are *invocation,* where we ask for the gifts of God's presence among us, and *confession,* where we acknowledge our sins and unworthiness and ask for God's forgiveness. *Intercession* is asking God to act on behalf of someone else.

In some services all these kinds of prayer may be combined into one long prayer, which some call the *pastoral prayer.* In other services there are several different prayers for different purposes. Many churches find that if there is only one prayer it tends to be mostly petitions and intercessions, with little thanksgiving and praise and even less confession. For this reason there is often a special prayer of confession, introduced by a call to confession and followed by a time of silence for personal reflection and then a declaration of pardon by the leader, which may quote words of assurance from the Bible and may involve an answering declaration of pardon by the people to the leader.

Many churches make provision in their prayers of petition, intercession, and thanksgiving for persons to express their prayer concerns. This may be done in various ways. In congregations and sanctuaries small enough that anyone can speak and be heard by everyone, persons may be invited to pray spontaneously in turn, expressing their concerns. Such prayers should be kept very brief, so as to give others a chance without unduly prolonging the prayer. Persons may be invited to express their prayer requests or concerns. The congregation may pray a response such as "Lord, hear our prayer" after each concern, or the leader may gather up these concerns into one prayer. In other congregations, especially if they are large, persons either make the leader aware of their concerns ahead of the service, perhaps through cards dropped into a prayer request box or added to a prayer request sheet, or use cards placed in their seats and pass them forward with the aid of the ushers during the service. The leader then incorporates these concerns into the prayers. Whatever method is used, sometimes there is a special time or effort to elicit the people's joys and thanksgivings, since otherwise the concerns may be largely sorrows and petitions.

There are special prayers and praises that are said or sung in unison every week. Although people who attend church regularly are likely to have memorized these, it is a gesture of welcome to strangers and others who may not know these acts of worship by heart to print them out in the bulletin or refer persons to where they may be found in the hymnal.

The chief of these is the Lord's Prayer, taught by Jesus to his disciples and found twice in the New Testament (Matthew 6:9-13 and Luke 11:2-4). It is the supreme Christian prayer and the summary of all Christian prayer, and most United Methodist churches include it in every Sunday service. For the convenience of those who do not know it by heart, it is printed in *The United Methodist Hymnal*, pages 894, 895, and 896, in each of the three translations widely used by United Methodists. Congregations may choose to sing it, using either of the versions of pages 270 and 271 of the hymnal.

The Doxology is also sung in many churches every week. The term *doxology* refers to any praise to the Trinity, and many of our hymns contain a doxology as their final stanza. A list of doxologies in our hymnal is found on page 951. The doxology commonly referred to as "The Doxology" is number 95 in our hymnal, and a contemporary version of it is number 94.

Also commonly sung each week is the *Gloria Patri* (Latin for "Glory to the Father"). The musical settings numbered 70 and 71 in our hymnal are both widely used by United Methodists.

You may be interested in learning more about these or any of the hymns in our hymnal. The sources and dates of both words and music are given in the hymnal below each hymn. The Index of Composers, Authors, and Sources (pages 914-923) gives additional information. In addition, the story behind each hymn is given in the book *The Hymns of The United Methodist Hymnal* (See For Further Reading).

CHAPTER 6

Proclamation and Response

God's Word

After the opening prayer and praise comes the main part of the Service of the Word, which we call "Proclamation and Response." This is the time when God's Word is proclaimed to the people and the people make appropriate responses.

We call the first part of the service, prior to Proclamation and Praise, the *Entrance*. This includes Gathering, Greeting, and Opening Prayers and Praise. We have responded to the call: "Come into God's presence with singing! . . . Enter God's gates with thanksgiving, and God's courts with praise!" (Psalm 100:2, 4; *UM Hymnal,* page 821).

The move from Entrance to Proclamation and Praise is a dramatic turning point in the service. Up to this point, while we have been aware that we were responding to God's prior call, the emphasis has been on our prayer and praise to God. Now the emphasis will be on God's Word for us and our response to the Word. This turning point is like that moment on the first Easter Day when the two disciples had finished pouring out their hearts and Jesus began quoting and interpreting the scriptures to them (Luke 24:25-27).

This turning point is often marked by a brief prayer in which we pray that the Holy Spirit may enlighten and empower the reading, preaching, hearing, and doing of God's Word. Such a prayer is often prayed by the preacher, but in some ways it is even more appropriate that a layperson lead this prayer. Many congregations pray this prayer in unison. If the Entrance is very brief, this invocation is often included in the opening prayer.

What do we mean by *God's Word*? It has three closely related meanings: God's Word written (scripture), God's Word preached (the sermon), and God's living Word (Jesus Christ). The reading and preaching of the Word are means by which the living Word (Christ) speaks to us.

The scriptures need to be opened to the people—that is, set before the people in such a way that their message is made plain and Christ can speak through them. Traditionally and most commonly this is done by reading passages of scripture and then preaching about part or all of the scriptures that have been read, but there are other ways in which this can be done. Scripture can sometimes be sung, dramatized by two or more persons, visualized through film or videotape, enhanced by sacred dance or interpretive movement, or witnessed to by persons who tell of their own experience. But since reading and preaching the scriptures are how they are usually proclaimed, let's look more closely at what happens when this is done.

Reading the Scriptures

Since ancient times the public reading of scripture has involved call and response.

There is a sense in which this is continually going on as scripture is read and preached. The people respond inwardly and let their responses show in their body language—the expressions on their faces, their postures, spontaneous nods and shakes of their heads. In many congregations it is customary to punctuate the preaching with responses like "amen" or "praise God" or "preach"—

sometimes so constantly that a high frequency call-and-response rhythm is apparent.

Since ancient times there has also been another slow frequency call-and-response rhythm as the reading of scripture is interspersed with acts of praise—psalms, anthems, hymns, or other responses. These responses of praise may be sung or spoken—in unison by the congregation, antiphonally between leader and people, between different parts of the congregation, or by choir or soloists. In any case, this is done by, or on behalf of, the whole congregation to express the congregation's response of praise to God for the message of God's Word.

Also, each scripture reading may begin or end with a set form of words that embodies a call and response. Thus, at the end of a reading the reader may say, "The Word of the Lord," and the people may respond, "Thanks be to God." Or the reader may say (his or her personal response of) "amen," after which the people may say their "amen."

In a growing number of congregations one or more of the scripture readings may be read by someone other than the preacher. This follows ancient custom and is one of the ways laypersons can effectively share in the leadership of worship. By the careful preparation of the reading and by their sense of the importance of the ministry they are performing, readers of scripture can make readings one of the high points of the service. It is both fair to all segments of the congregation and also more interesting and effective if the readers chosen over a period of time represent, in fair proportions, women and men, youth and young adults as well as middle-aged and older adults, and whatever ethnic and cultural variety is in the congregation.

The reading of scripture is seen as well as heard, and there are ways of making it visually effective. At the beginning of the service, or just before the scriptures are to be read, the Bible that is to be read from may be ceremonially carried to the pulpit, either processionally down the aisle or from wherever the Bible may have been during the week. In other churches the Bible sits open on the pulpit at all times as a symbol of the function of the pulpit as the place from which God's Word is read and preached. A large pulpit Bible signifies by both its size and imposing appearance the importance of scripture, and it also has print large enough for easy reading.

There has been a growing tendency in recent years to read more scripture. At least two passages, and often three, are read in an increasing proportion of churches at each Sunday service. This recovers traditional practice and is especially helpful today when the only scripture many persons ever see or hear is what is read in the weekly service. When two or three readings are used, it is not necessary that the preacher deal with all of them in the sermon. God's Word can be communicated by an act of reading done well.

There has been a related trend toward systematically covering the story and message of the Bible over a period of time in a given congregation. If this is not done, it is easy for the preacher to "ride hobby horses" and repeatedly read and preach from certain favorite passages.

The most commonly used system of covering the basics of scripture is the Lectionary, a three-year cycle of suggested scripture readings developed by scholars of many denominations and now used throughout the world by churches of numerous denominations. This lectionary offers several advantages. Pastors have become convinced that it does a better job of covering the story and message of the Bible than any plan they could devise, particularly given the busy schedules of pastors today. A large number of published helps for planning worship and preparing sermons follow the lectionary, and in many communities two or more clergy get together each week to share insights and ideas regarding the scriptures in the following Sunday's lectionary. In many congregations the scripture readings are distributed to the congregation in advance for private reading, for weekly Bible study groups, and for the benefit of musicians and others who have a part in planning services.

Of course, use of the lectionary is not an all-or-nothing matter. Some pastors see the lectionary as their starting point and then feel free to substitute other scriptures as circumstances in the life of the congregation may warrant. Still other pastors systematically preach through the Bible by a plan they themselves have devised. You might ask your pastor, if you do not already know, what plan she or he uses for covering the story and teachings of the Bible.

The Psalms are also being recovered as the most basic and traditional hymnal or collection of acts of praise that Christians have. Examine the Psalter on pages 735-862 of our hymnal and also chapter 7 on this Psalter in *The Worship Resources of The United Methodist Hymnal* (See For Further Reading). Reflect on the ways in which your congregation uses this Psalter—or could learn to use it. You may wish to investigate how many of the anthems and hymns that your congregation uses take their words from the Bible, and especially from the Psalms. You will find the Index of Scripture on pages 924-26 helpful.

The Sermon

The reading of scripture and related acts of praise lead to the sermon and to the response called for by the sermon.

The sermon occupies the central place in most United Methodist worship services. The average United Methodist pastor probably receives more training in sermon preparation and delivery than in any other phase of worship planning and leadership. He or she probably spends more time each week in sermon preparation than in all other forms of worship preparation combined.

As you listen to the preaching, it helps to have in mind some basic questions. What is the preacher trying to do? What does the preacher want to happen in your life as a result? What do *you* want to happen? Is there some situation in your life in which you need help?

It is hard to be specific in a book like this about the preaching in your particular congregation because preaching is by its very nature tailor-made to a particular situation—to the particular gifts of your pastor and to the particular needs of your congregation. It may be helpful to discuss with your pastor how he or she views the purpose of preaching, prepares and structures sermons, and works for responses to the Word. It may also be helpful to share with your pastor what you feel you need to hear in preaching.

But the ultimate question is not what *the preacher* wants, or what *you* want, but what *God* wants you to hear and do. You may hear something that the preacher wasn't aware of saying and didn't intend, but which can be God's Word to you and which can change your life. You may hear something that causes you to feel a need or a hunger you had never been aware of. Even if your mind has been wandering, suddenly you may hear something that gives you an insight that is God's gift to you—though this may be far from what the preacher had in mind. When the preacher is faithfully reading and preaching the Bible, there is much more in preaching than even the preacher is aware of.

What Do You Do After the Sermon?

Preaching is a call in search of a response. Whether or not there is a formal invitation to Christian discipleship following the sermon, a sermon itself ought to be an invitation to Christian commitment.

The ultimate response to God's Word is the character of our Christian faith and life day by day, but an immediate response is also important. If we simply walk out of church after the sermon without doing anything to affirm our *commitment* to what has been proclaimed then we have missed an opportunity to do something that would strengthen us as we go back to be Christians in our daily world.

Preachers often end their sermons with the call, "Let us pray," after which they lead the congregation in a prayer that expresses the hoped-for response. Ideally, each person makes this prayer a personal act of commitment and signifies this by adding a personal "amen." The danger is that this prayer will be experienced as simply an extension of the sermon and a solo act of the minister.

A stronger response is a hymn following the sermon in which the congregation expresses its commitment and faith. This hymn may be chosen because it expresses a response appropriate to the sermon just preached, or it may be a general hymn of praise and thanksgiving.

In many churches there is an invitation to Christian discipleship following the sermon and before what may be called the invitation hymn. During this hymn, whose words may express both call and response, persons may come forward to profess or reaffirm their faith in Christ, to be baptized or present children for baptism, to be confirmed, or to join the church by transfer.

Sometimes the invitation is expressed more broadly so that persons may also respond with acts such as giving a personal witness, making some response to the sermon, or making a commitment to a particular form of Christian service or a particular course of action.

Many churches use a creed or affirmation of faith as a congregational response to the Word. While an affirmation of faith can occur at various points in the service, it is especially appropriate as a response to the Word because it is an expression of our commitment and faith. The Apostles' Creed, which is the affirmation most commonly used by United Methodists, originated in the early church as a profession of faith for those presenting themselves for baptism and is appropriate not only at baptisms but at any service as a reminder of the faith into which we have been baptized. You may wish to study the affirmations of faith in our hymnal (880-89) and the background of each affirmation on pages 199-203 of *The Worship Resources of The United Methodist Hymnal* (See For Further Reading).

Increasingly the period of concerns and prayers is placed after the sermon as a response to the Word. This follows the pattern described by Justin Martyr in the second century (see page 18 above) and enables us in the light of the Word that has been proclaimed to make more specific our commitment to God and to the needs of others.

The character of the service or of the preaching may make a congregational prayer of confession followed by a declaration of pardon an appropriate response.

The offering of money and gifts for the work of the church or for the needy is often placed after the sermon as a response to the Word, a symbol of our larger offering of ourselves and all that we have in God's service. The offering can be received at various points in the service, and its placement helps to determine its significance as an act of worship. Even if it is earlier in the service, however, it may be intended to symbolize our commitment in response to the call that has preceded it. A key symbolic moment in many offering ceremonies occurs when the ushers, who have received the offering from the people, bring it forward and place it—or give it to one of the leaders of worship to place—on the Lord's table as prayer or praise is spoken or sung.

At some point in the service the people in many congregations exchange with each other words and gestures of God's peace. The Peace is an act of reconciliation and blessing, based on the practice of the New Testament Christians (Romans 16:16; 1 Corinthians 16:20; 2 Corinthians 13:2; 1 Thessalonians 5:26; 1 Peter 5:14). It should not be confused with the Ritual of Friendship (see page 38 above). In the Peace, we bless our neighbors with the peace of Christ and signify that we are at peace with them in the spirit of Christ. If it comes immediately before the Offering, particularly if it follows the Confession and Pardon, we may recall Matthew 5:23-24.

In services when Holy Communion is celebrated, the Invitation, Confession and Pardon, Peace and Offering are commonly a bridge between the Service of the Word, where they function as a response, and Holy Communion, for which they are a preparation. It is fitting that we turn now to Holy Communion.

CHAPTER 7

Holy Communion

The Basic Pattern

We have already seen that in the historic pattern of Christian Sunday worship the Service of the Word is followed by Holy Communion—also called the *Lord's Supper* (1 Corinthians 11:20), the *Breaking of Bread* (Acts 2:42), the Eucharist (from the New Testament Greek word for thanksgiving), or the Service of the Table. For most Christians and during most of church history, Holy communion has been inseparable from the Service of the Word. The two together have formed the main Sunday service of the church.

For most United Methodist congregations today, the weekly worship only occasionally includes Holy Communion—perhaps monthly, sometimes quarterly, and sometimes on certain special occasions in the church year. This is ironic since our founder John Wesley urged his followers to receive communion every week. In recent years an increasing number of United Methodist churches have been making Holy Communion available every week, if not at the main Sunday service then at some other time in the week.

On pages 6-31 of our new hymnal there are several Services of Word and Table that help United Methodists celebrate Holy Communion. A choice of services is offered so that Holy Communion may be longer or briefer, formal or informal, in traditional or modern language, adapted to the day or season, and in a variety of musical styles, depending on the requirements of a particular congregation or situation.

Let's suppose that you are taking part in congregational worship on an occasion when Holy Communion is being celebrated. The Service of the Word has been completed, and the Service of the Table (Holy Communion) is beginning. What is going on?

The Bible makes it clear that Holy Communion is a *meal*—the Lord's Supper. It is breaking bread and drinking from the cup with the living, risen Jesus Christ and with our sisters and brothers in Christ at the Lord's table. The living Christ is hosting us just as surely as when he ate with those first disciples while he preached and healed in Galilee and Judea, when he ate with them on the night before he gave his life for us, and when he was recognized by the disciples in those first resurrection meals.

We have seen that since the earliest years of the Christian church this holy meal has usually been a token meal of bread and wine rather than a full-course meal, but this does not change the fact that it is a meal. Our everyday lives are full of token meals that fulfill the communal purposes of eating and drinking together on occasions when we neither need nor want to eat a full meal. The Lord's Supper is, of course, a very special and holy kind of meal; but we can understand its special and holy character better if we keep in mind that it is a meal.

Because it is a meal, Holy Communion is basically a series of actions in which words, while essential, are less prominent. As we look at the New Testament meals that are our models for Holy Communion, we find four simple actions. Following Jesus' own actions, we in his name (1) take the bread and cup, (2) give thanks (say a blessing) over the bread and cup, (3) break the bread, and (4) give the bread and cup to one another. (See Matthew 26:26-28; Mark 14:22-23; Luke 22:17-20, 24:30; and 1 Corinthians 11:23-25.) While words may be spoken during any of these steps, it is only the second step (giving thanks) that is primarily a matter of words. Since the first and third of these actions are brief and preliminary to the second and fourth, we may group these actions into two: (1) taking the bread and cup and giving thanks over them, and (2) breaking the bread and giving the bread and cup to one another. These two steps may be referred to simply as Thanksgiving and Communion.

First, the pastor (or some other ordained minister) takes the bread and cup. The bread and wine (grape juice) are brought to the Lord's table, or uncovered if already in place. Churches today are increasingly using a large uncut loaf of real bread, following the practice reported in 1 Corinthians 10:16-17. As Paul tells us, the one loaf powerfully symbolizes the fact that we are one body in Christ. Use of a large common cup, a *chalice,* is also a powerful symbol of our unity in Christ, although for sanitary reasons most United Methodists use small individual cups or dip their bread in the common cup rather than drinking from it. Since the late nineteenth century, when pasteurized grape juice became available, the great majority of congregations in what is now The United Methodist Church have used unfermented grape juice for the communion wine as an expression of concern for recovering alcoholics, as a support for the practice of abstinence, and in order to include children and youth.

Then, just as we give thanks over our food and drink when it is brought to the table at home, so we do at the Lord's table. The pastor says a very special and traditional blessing known as the Great Thanksgiving, which includes responses said or sung by the people. This prayer expresses in words what we are doing when we celebrate Holy Communion. Studying the words of the Great Thanksgiving in the hymnal (pages 9-11, 13-14, 27-30) is a great help in understanding Holy Communion. The pastor first gives appropriate thanks to God, recalling God's acts of salvation through Jesus Christ and the institution of the Lord's Supper by Christ himself. Then the pastor prays that what we offer to God may be joined with Christ's offering for us, invokes the power of the Holy Spirit, and sometimes makes intercessions for God's people. The people respond by singing or saying, "Holy, Holy, Holy Lord" and the Memorial Acclamation "Christ has died, Christ is risen, Christ will come again." The prayer traditionally ends with a doxology (praise to the Trinity) and the people sing or say what is known as the Great Amen.

Following the Great Thanksgiving it is traditional to pray the Lord's Prayer as a bridge between the Thanksgiving and the Communion. The Lord's Prayer is both the sublime climax of our thanksgiving to God and a verbal entrance into a communion with God that is holy and intimate beyond words.

The Communion includes breaking the bread and giving the bread and cup. The pastor continues to preside but is often assisted by others in distributing the bread and wine.

The ancient practice of first breaking the uncut loaf by hand is being restored in United Methodist congregations. The cup may also be raised as a gesture of invitation to partake. This may be done in silence or accompanied by appropriate words such as those of Paul in 1 Corinthians 10:16-17, which is the passage on which our use of the term *Communion* is based. Paul writes that the bread which we break is a *koinonia* in the body of Christ, and that the cup over which we give thanks is a _koinonia,_ in the blood of Christ. The New Testament Greek word _koinonia_ may be translated "communion," "fellowship," "participation," "sharing," or "intimate relationship." In the ancient world it was a favorite word for the relationship of husband and wife. It describes our relationship both with Christ and with one another in Christ.

The bread and cup may be given to the people in various ways. The people may come forward and receive them standing, sitting, or kneeling. They may be passed while the people remain in their seats, or with the people standing in a circle if it is a small congregation. In any case, the pastor continues to preside but may be assisted by others in giving the bread and cup. This is the climax of the whole service, the act that unites us to the living Christ and to the whole communion of saints in heaven and on earth. This act constitutes, or reconstitutes, us as the body of Christ, the church. Often during the giving of the bread and cup the people sing hymns, gospel songs, and choruses that express the intimacy and joy of our union with Christ and with one another. This is a good time to sing the most familiar and beloved songs, preferably ones that the people know by heart or can readily learn by rote without having to use a hymnal.

What follows giving the bread and cup is usually brief, a reentry into a more ordinary plane of life. The Lord's table is put in order. There is usually a brief prayer of thanksgiving after Communion (like thanking one's host after a meal). A hymn may be sung (Matthew 26:30; Mark 4:26), which may serve as the thanksgiving after communion. The people are sent forth into the world with a blessing _(benediction)._ The communion bread and wine may be taken afterward to the sick and others unable to attend, or some other reverent disposition may be made of them.

The Meanings of Holy Communion

What does it all mean? Thousands of books have been written through the centuries and throughout the world on the many meanings of Holy Communion. Several of these are listed under For Further Reading at the end of this book. If what this act means could be put into words, then the act itself might be unnecessary and we could content ourselves with the words. Words can only point in the direction of what can be conveyed by the experience itself, and even the experience grows and changes as we do. One facet of meaning will be most important to one person, another facet to another person.

The fact that this act is referred to by a variety of names suggests that each name adds some facet of meaning. The term *Holy Communion* shows the holiness and intimacy of the union with Christ and his body (the church) that this act creates and expresses. *Lord's Supper* shows that it is a meal hosted by our Lord. *Eucharist* shows the spirit of thanksgiving that permeates it. *Sacrament,* from the Latin term for a soldier's pledge of allegiance, shows that it is both Christ's pledge of commitment to us and our pledge of commitment to Christ and his church. *Ordinance* shows that it has been instituted and ordained for us by Christ.

All kinds of statements, each true as far as it goes, can be made about the symbolism of the bread and cup and what we do with them.

Breaking the bread and pouring the wine represent the breaking of Jesus' body and the pouring out of his blood on the cross—and more! They represent the giving and pouring out of his total life and ministry—his birth, life and teaching, suffering and death, resurrection and ascension, presence today, and final victory.

Giving the bread and cup to everyone present proclaims

Jesus' giving of himself for everyone. The dividing and sharing of the bread and cup demonstrate our stewardship not only of the gospel but of all God's gifts, including the fruits and resources of the earth. They are to be shared with all people, just as we share the bread and wine with the whole congregation.

Receiving the bread and cup from the hand of another person represents our receiving God's love in Christ, which comes to us through other persons. Giving and receiving food have always been primary ways in which people have given and received love. As we taste and see the bread and wine, we remember the words of Psalm 34:8: "Taste and see that the LORD is good."

Sharing the one loaf of bread as we repeat Jesus' words, "This is my body," is indeed a participation *(koinonia)* in the one body of Christ.

Drinking from the cup as we repeat Jesus' words, "This is my blood, which seals God's covenant" (Matthew 26:28 TEV) does indeed renew our covenant relationship with God, sealed once and for all by the shedding of Christ's blood.

Moreover, this "cup of blessing" represents life. The Bible repeatedly identifies blood with life (Genesis 9:4; Leviticus 17:11; Deuteronomy 12:23). By sharing this cup we share in the *life* of the living Christ. Receiving the cup renews the life of Christ in us.

Holy Communion not only unites the past and present, it anticipates the future. We eat and drink this "until he comes" in final victory (1 Corinthians 11:26). This token of food and drink, like the token food served by a host before the dinner is ready, is not only a foretaste of heaven for each of us, it is also a foretaste of the messianic banquet when Christ will have won his ultimate victory.

We could go on indefinitely with such interpretations. Each is a perspective from which we can see part of the whole meaning of Holy Communion. Those who find one perspective most helpful do not have to argue with, much less separate from, those who find another perspective most helpful. Christians have argued and fought over just how Christ is present, how the bread and wine are changed, how the service should be conducted, who is authorized to preside at it, and who is eligible to receive the bread and cup. Surely this family meal of Jesus' disciples should bring us together in love, not keep us apart!

Ultimately, the Holy Communion that we have with God in Jesus Christ is a mystery. The Bible speaks of "the mystery of the gospel" (Ephesians 6:19), "the mystery of the faith" (1 Timothy 3:9), "the mystery of our religion" (1 Timothy 3:16), "the mystery of Christ" (Colossians 4:3), "this mystery, which is Christ in you, the hope of glory" (Colossians 1:27), "the mystery of God" (Revelation 10:7). We are "stewards of the mysteries of God" (1 Corinthians 4:1). When a pastor or other ordained minister presides at this holy meal, no matter how much theological education and spiritual maturity he or she may have, this sacred responsibility that has been entrusted to him or her is that of a steward who passes on something that goes beyond the understanding of any of us. God may reveal to you in Holy Communion something that the pastor did not intend or was not aware of, and that's all right. None of us is so wise as to have plumbed the depths of the mystery.

On the other hand, the mystery of the gospel is revealed even to young children—*especially* to young children, if we remember Jesus' words (Mark 10:13-16). A small child who eats and drinks at this holy meal already knows the difference between being included at a meal table and excluded from it and already connects being fed with being loved. Recognizing that children are part of Christ's family, United Methodists increasingly welcome them to Christ's family meal. Through this holy meal God can reveal the mystery of the gospel to children at whatever their stage of development.

In fact, as we get older our theories and explanations sometimes get in the way of God revealing more of the mystery to us. If somewhere in the process of growing up you learned some set formula to explain Holy Communion, you may not realize that your understanding did not begin with that formula and will not end with it. On the other hand, if you have difficulty participating in Holy Communion—or even stay away—because it doesn't make sense to you or because some interpretation you once heard is incredible or offensive, perhaps the interpretation you once heard should be put aside in favor of one more suited to your present state of maturity or in favor of more openness to the mystery.

Many persons have stayed away from Holy Communion over the years because they misinterpreted Paul's warning: "Whoever, therefore, eats the bread or drinks the cup of the Lord in an unworthy manner will be answerable for the body and blood of the Lord. . . . For all who eat and drink without discerning the body, eat and drink judgment against themselves" (1 Corinthians 11:27, 29). If we read the whole passage (verses 17-34), we discover that Paul was referring to a situation in the church at Corinth where persons were bringing their own food and drink and sometimes eating and drinking to excess while refusing to share with those who had brought nothing and were going hungry. Those selfish persons were obviously communing in an unworthy manner. They failed to discern the body of Christ—the hungry people right there in front of them who were members of Christ's body. They were shutting themselves off from the Christ who was in "the least of these" (Matthew 25:31-46).

Paul's warning has nothing to do with the level on which we can intellectually understand Holy Communion. If we can be glad for the blessing that Christ gives not only to children but also to persons of all ages who are mentally limited, we can be glad that Christ's invitation includes us, regardless of our level of understanding.

Paul's warning also has nothing to do with our present level of moral development, providing we come willing to let Christ raise us from wherever we are—whether we are the worst sinner or the greatest saint—to something higher. Receiving communion in a worthy manner is not at all the same as receiving communion because we think we are worthy. The only way any of us is worthy is through God's gift in Christ, and to come to the Lord's table because we thought we had earned the right to be there would in itself be an unworthy motive. Christ has always been known as one who liked to eat with sinners (Luke 15:2), and he still does.

So come to the table and let Christ feed you food to grow on.

CHAPTER 8

Day by Day

Back into Daily Life

Whether or not there has been Holy Communion, the service usually ends with acts that send us out into the everyday world.

A closing hymn—sometimes with a recession by pastor, other leaders, and choir—may express and strengthen our sense that we are going into the world as Christians.

There is usually a dismissal with a blessing in the name of the Trinity, given by the pastor and often called the *Benediction.* In its traditional form it is *not* a prayer; it is spoken to the people face-to-face. It is therefore appropriate to keep your eyes open and look at the pastor, since she or he is talking to you.

The service of congregational worship continues as long as people are still with others in the place of worship. Just as the Gathering is part of the service, so is the Going Forth. Organ or other instrumental music may be played in a spirit of joyous praise. In some congregations the people remain seated and listen, in others the people go out during the music, and still in other congregations the people feel free either to remain seated or go out as the music is played. People may stand around and talk for awhile, either in or immediately outside the church building, before scattering. Others may wish to leave quickly and quietly.

We scatter into the world of our daily life, better rehearsed for the living of the coming week as a result of our worship. During the week the persons "on stage" with us will have attended "rehearsals" other than the one in our local church or none at all. God the Playwright will still be present, but we shall need to be perceptive if we are to keep in touch.

Constant communion with God and feeling the constant support of other Christians when we are not face-to-face is a sublime ideal. It can increasingly become a fact as we grow in the Christian faith and life. It becomes possible to perceive God's leading in all kinds of events day by day. More and more we can find ourselves spontaneously praying exclamations, phrases, sentences silently—perhaps even aloud—to the God who is always with us. We can internalize Scripture so that passages come to mind when needed. What we sing in church can come to our hearts, if not our lips, as our song whenever the Spirit moves. All meals can be a holy mystery, and even when we eat alone we can know the presence of the communion of saints.

But let's face it, most of us are a long way from this ideal. If we are to move in this direction it needs to be step by step, and this means structure—a structure of time and perhaps a structure of place as well. Some persons need more structure than others. We all need some mixture of structure and freedom.

We have already seen how important the structuring of time is in Christian life and worship. The structure of the week is important. The internal structure and the rhythm of the worship service are important.

Likewise, the structure of the day is important—to our life and to our worship.

Most of us have some kind of daily cycle and structure. Unlike the cycle or the week or the rhythm of a worship service, the cycle of day and night is given in nature. Unless we are in the Arctic or Antarctic, there is a structure of the day and night every twenty-four hours. If you have ever spent a long time in a windowless room or underground, you know how disorienting it can be not to experience the rhythm of day and night. The time of day is also important. Most people structure their days around such times as getting up and going to bed, going to and from work or school, mealtimes, break times, times to have fun, times for favorite television shows.

Daily Worship

What has all this to do with worship? A great deal. If our relationship to Christ and his family is to make any difference day to day and not be something we forget about from Sunday to Sunday, we need some pattern of daily worship. The traditions of daily worship that have persisted among Christians through the centuries have taken advantage of existing structures. There are long and rich traditions of morning and evening prayer, both in the form of personal and family devotions and in large gatherings. Sometimes there are both evening prayer at the end of the working day and night prayer before sleep. Even the heritage in monasteries of prayer at three-hour intervals, which seems incredibly removed from life as most of us know it, is strikingly parallel to what many of us experience in such common daily rituals as getting up, breakfast, going to work, midmorning break, lunch, midafternoon break, return home, dinner, and going to bed.

Structures of place and support systems of people may also help during the week. If your church means a great deal to you, it may help you to return to church for services or meetings between Sunday mornings. There may be a special place at home or at work where you find it easier to reflect and get in touch. You may belong to a small group that meets regularly, includes forms of worship such as Bible study and prayer, shares faith and experiences with one another, and may have some sort of agreement as to personal daily Bible reading and prayer. You may engage in Bible reading, prayer, singing, or other devotional practices as a family.

Since this book is about public worship, this is not the place to enter into a discussion of personal, family, and small-group worship. These are of great importance in themselves, and other books deal with them. What is important to note here is that daily worship, even if not usually done in a congregational setting, is nurtured by Sunday worship services and in turn becomes the foundation upon which Sunday worship is supported and grows.

Another way we are nurtured in daily worship is by the model of daily worship that we experience at a church conference of almost any sort, particularly one that extends overnight. Such conferences, camps, retreats—whatever they may be called—commonly mark the turning points of the day by some form of worship. There is probably a morning service in which singing and prayers celebrate the beginning of another day. At the end of the afternoon or at the end of the evening, or at both times, there is probably a service when praise and prayer remind us that the sun has set and evening or night has come. Other turning points in the day such as meals or reconvening after a recess may be marked by a hymn or a brief prayer.

Some congregations are situated where they can offer brief morning, noon, or evening services for persons on their way to or from work or during lunch hour. Some schools, particularly theological seminaries, have daily services and may, in addition, open class sessions with prayer. Such services commonly contain references to the time of day.

In churches where this is not feasible every day it is often done on Sunday and perhaps once in the middle of the week. Morning prayer and the singing of morning hymns are often features of the first part of Sunday morning worship, or there may be a short prayer service before the main Sunday service. Saturday or Sunday evening services take advantage of the fact that in the evening most persons are more open and expressive, particularly at the level of their feelings, than they are earlier in the day. Evening hymns may be sung. Midweek morning and evening services are likely to take on the character of the time of day in which they are held.

Many are finding the Orders of Daily Praise and Prayer on pages 876-79 of the hymnal to be a help in structuring weekday worship in any or all of these various forms.

Corporate worship services may provide models that help us structure our daily personal or family worship. Giving thanks (saying a blessing) and perhaps other acts of worship at meals can remind us of the sacredness of eating together and can be an occasion to note the turning of the time of day and a time to remember family and others who are not physically present. Many persons set aside a quiet time—when they first get up, before they begin the day's work, at some break such as the lunch hour, at the end of work, or at the end of the evening. This may be the briefest moment, or it may be longer if possible. Persons who find themselves waking in the middle of the night sometimes find it helpful to mark these times with a momentary prayer.

If there is a special need today in daily worship, it may be to recover more use of Scripture. Daily worship at its best includes some plan—and there are many good plans—for reading through the Bible. The Psalms in particular have been at the heart of daily worship throughout Christian history, and the historic traditions of Christian daily worship make extensive use of the Psalms every day. You may find the format in which the Psalms are presented on pages 735-862 of the hymnal to be helpful. In fact, if there is one great secret to bringing daily prayer to life, it is knowing and using the Psalms and making their incredibly open and honest style of prayer and praise our own.

CHAPTER 9

The Christian Year

The Rhythm of the Year

The weekdays have gone by, and now it's Sunday again. The cycle of another week begins. One Sunday follows another, and we learn to ask "*Which* Sunday is it?" Which Sunday in the season? Which Sunday in the year? The Lord's Day is not only the foundation of the Christian week, it is also the foundation of the Christian year.

As there is a rapid and continuous rhythm of call and response going on every moment of our worship, a less rapid rhythm of call and response by which the acts of worship in a service of worship are arranged, a slower rhythm of times of day and night, and a still slower rhythm that structures the week around the Lord's Day, so there is a rhythm in the sequence of Lord's Days that gives structure to the Christian year.

The rhythm of the Christian year has its roots in the Bible, took its basic shape in the early church, and has continued to develop over the centuries.

The Easter Cycle

We read in the Bible how the people of ancient Israel observed a variety of yearly festivals that related both to the agriculture that structured their lives and to the events in their history that constituted their story as a people. It was very significant to Jesus and his first disciples that he was crucified at Passover time, when Jews were commemorating how God had delivered their ancestors from slavery in Egypt, brought them safely through the Red Sea, and made them a free people. We, too, these earliest Christians realized, have been delivered by God and are no longer slaves to sin and death. We have been made a free people through the suffering, death, and resurrection of Christ. Referring to the lamb that was sacrificed at Passover, Paul said: "Our paschal [Passover] lamb, Christ, has been sacrificed. Therefore, let us celebrate the festival" (1 Corinthians 5:7-8).

And so, although the early Christians celebrated God's saving work in Christ every Lord's Day, it seemed fitting when Passover time came around each year that there be some sort of great yearly Lord's Day as the Christian Passover. Christians were observing this *Pascha* (Passover) at least as early as the second century and possibly even in New Testament times.

Its climax was the baptizing of new Christians, followed by Holy Communion, which for the first time included these new Christians as members of the body of Christ. Baptism was seen as being delivered through water into freedom in Christ, like the delivery of Israel through the Red Sea. It was burial and resurrection with Christ (Romans 6:4-5).

There had to be preparation for such a solemn act. Hippolytus, writing in the third century, tells that those to be baptized fasted on Friday and Saturday and then took part in a vigil all Saturday night. Sunday morning at cockcrow, the hour when Christ was said to have risen from the dead, they were baptized beneath the waters and rose with Christ as from the dead.

During the fourth century the *Pascha* was divided into several observances spread over several days. The institution of the Lord's Supper was commemorated on Thursday evening, Jesus' death on Friday, and his resurrection on Saturday night and Sunday morning. These observances became Holy Thursday, Good Friday, and Easter. The word *Easter,* used in English-speaking countries, comes from the Anglo-Saxon *Eastre,* the name of a pre-Christian goddess and her spring festival. Other languages such as French, Spanish, and Italian still use words derived from *Pascha,* which make it evident that we are celebrating the Christian Passover. The Great Three Days from sunset Holy Thursday through Easter Day are still the climax of the Christian year.

Also in the fourth century the week before Easter began to be observed as Holy Week, beginning with the Sunday we know as Passion/Palm Sunday, when Jesus' entry into Jerusalem and subsequent passion (suffering) are commemorated. The early weekdays of Holy Week have always been of less importance, however, than the Great Three Days.

You may have wondered why Easter falls on a different date each year. Like the Jewish Passover, it is determined by the phases of the moon. Early Christians debated the proper date for the *Pascha* and agreed in the fourth century that it, unlike the Jewish Passover, must always be celebrated on a Sunday so that the weekly and yearly celebrations of Jesus' resurrection reinforce each other. Later in western Europe it came to be observed on the Sunday after the first full moon on or after March 21, which can place Easter as early as March 22 or as late as April 25. This is how Protestants and Roman Catholics still date Easter.

Easter is more than a day; it is a season, which the early

Christians called the Great Fifty Days, beginning with Easter Day and extending through Pentecost on the fiftieth day (seven Sundays) following. It commemorates the fifty days that began when Jesus rose from the dead and ended when the Holy Spirit came upon the disciples and the Christian church was born. This season, already well established by the third century, is like a great fifty-day Lord's Day. It was seen by the early Christians as being to the year what the Lord's Day was to the week—the first one-seventh of the time, when we celebrate what God has done through Christ. Easter, then, is a day of the week, a day of the year, and a season of the year.

Since ancient times it has been a trinitarian celebration. It has been celebrated as the season of God's creation and new creation—especially appropriate in parts of the world where this season is also spring. It has been not only the commemoration of Jesus' resurrection but the season of the living and ever-present Christ. It has been the season framed by the givings of the Holy Spirit on the first Easter Day (John 20:21-23) and on the day of Pentecost seven weeks later (Acts 2:1-4), in which we celebrate the gifts and fruits of the Spirit.

The emphasis on the Holy Spirit reaches its climax on the fiftieth and last day of the season, the day of Pentecost, which brings the Easter season to a glorious close. The term *Pentecost* is derived from the Greek words meaning "fiftieth" and "fifty." It was the name Greek-speaking Jews gave to the Jewish Day of First Fruits, or Feast of Weeks *(Shabuoth)*, the harvest festival commanded in Leviticus 23:16. It was the conclusion of the cycle that began at Passover, and the term *Pentecost* was also used to refer to the whole cycle. The early Christians, likewise, used the term *Pentecost* to refer not only to the day of Pentecost but also to the Great Fifty Days as a whole.

It has been significant for Christians that it was on the Jewish day of Pentecost that the Christian church was born. Sometime in the first century the day of Pentecost became for Jews not only a harvest festival but also a commemoration of the giving of the Torah (teaching, law) on Mount Sinai. Whether or not this had occurred by the time the account in Acts 2 was written, Christians from early times have drawn the parallel between the giving of the Torah and the giving of the Holy Spirit. Possibly even Paul was relating the two Pentecosts in 2 Corinthians 3:7-8. As God brought covenant with Israel to fruition on Mount Sinai, so God brought covenant with the disciples of Christ to fruition at Pentecost.

The day of Pentecost, at least as early as the second century, was a time when the church baptized candidates who had not been ready at Easter. Pentecost has always seemed an appropriate day for baptisms. Acts 2:41 records that on the day of Pentecost about three thousand persons were baptized. The day we celebrate the birth of the church is surely a fitting time to celebrate the spiritual birth of a Christian. From ancient times, Christians have thought of the gathering in of converts as like a harvest (Matthew 9:37-38; Luke 10:2; John 4:35) and have naturally thought of the Great Fifty Days with its harvest origins in ancient Israel as our great spiritual harvest season.

At first the day of Pentecost was a celebration of Jesus' ascension (Acts 1:1-11) as well as of the giving of the Holy Spirit (Acts 2). By the end of the fourth century, Christians had begun to celebrate Ascension as a separate festival on the fortieth day of the Easter season, remembering the references in Acts 1:3 to the forty-day period between Jesus' resurrection and ascension. Ascension Day falls on the Thursday following the sixth Sunday of the Easter season.

United Methodist congregations that celebrate the Ascension usually do so the following Sunday.

The Easter season soon came to be seen as requiring a season of preparation. This season, known as Lent, began in the early church as a period of final preparation and examination for those to be baptized at Easter. They had already undergone a long period of preparation and were now ready for the final scrutinies, as they were called. The length of this final preparatory period as being forty days was first mentioned in the early fourth century. The forty days came to be seen as comparable to Jesus' forty days in the wilderness, when he fasted and prepared himself for his ministry. By the fifth century, Lent was understood as a time of preparation by *all* Christians for the renewal of the whole church at Easter. Fasting, as a means to the spiritual discipline needed by Christians, was an important part of Lent. This made Lent a rather somber and strenuous season. Sometimes the emphasis has been negative—self-denial for its own sake. This is one reason some Protestants have reacted against observing Lent. At other times, and increasingly today, the emphasis has been positive—preparation for the Easter renewal of our Christian commitment.

Even in Lent every Lord's Day is a little Easter in which we encounter the risen Christ and celebrate his victory. The fact that it is the Lord's Day is more important than the fact that it is the season of Lent. For this reason, the six Sundays in Lent are not counted as part of the forty days. Lent thus has a total of forty-six days, beginning with Ash Wednesday (the seventh Wednesday before Easter) and concluding at sunset the day before Easter.

The seasons of Lent and Easter together, from Ash Wednesday through the day of Pentecost, are called the Easter Cycle—a great time of renewal each year in which the church and its members are challenged to move "from ashes to fire."

With all this history in mind, look at what happens in your local church during the Easter Cycle.

Partly your congregation will be commemorating key events in the life of Christ—his forty days in the wilderness and subsequent ministry, his entry into Jerusalem and suffering there, his institution of the Lord's Supper, his death, his resurrection, his ascension, and the coming of the Holy Spirit.

But this can be merely history except as it is linked with what is happening here and now. During the Easter Cycle persons are probably baptized, or confirmed, or received into your church by transfer or by reaffirmation of their faith. Prior to these ceremonies the candidates are probably instructed, as may be necessary, in the meaning of Christian faith and church membership. Following these ceremonies is a crucial time for assimilating these new members into your congregation (the body of Christ). Furthermore, the whole congregation (body) needs to be prepared for the "grafting in" of these new members if the process is to "take." Lent is a time when congregations and their members are likely to be challenged, both in worship, in classes, and in small groups, to commitment and growth in Christian faith and life. A growing number of churches are reviving the ancient Easter Vigil, either Saturday night or at sunrise, with its focus on Christian baptism and renewal.

Congregations that in the past have let everything slack off after Easter Day are rediscovering the joy of the Great Fifty Days. The Sundays of the Easter season, leading to Ascension (day or Sunday) and the day of Pentecost, can be jubilant celebrations with the risen Christ in the power of the Holy Spirit. Choirs and other creative and talented persons, if they do not exhaust themselves during Holy

Week, can see that music and other arts are at their most glorious during the Great Fifty Days. Classes and groups that begin in Lent can continue until the day of Pentecost.

What does going "from ashes to fire" mean—what might it mean—in your congregation?

The Christmas Cycle

The other great high period of the Christian year is the time of Christmas—the Christmas Cycle. Its origins in Christian history are not quite as early as those of the Easter Cycle, nor are they rooted in the festivals of ancient Israel. But so meaningful have Christmas and all that surrounds it become to Christian people that Christmas has joined Easter as one of the two peaks of the Christian year.

The feast of Epiphany is not as well known as Christmas, but it is older and was even more important in early Christian history. It falls on January 6, although United Methodist congregations that celebrate it usually do so on the first Sunday of January. The word *epiphany* means "manifestation." In Christian use it refers particularly to the manifestation of God in Jesus Christ—in his birth and baptism, in various events later in his ministry, and at last when he will come in final victory. The Christian feast of Epiphany probably began in Egypt, at least as early as the late second century.

At first, both the birth and the baptism of Jesus were celebrated on Epiphany, but during the fourth century it, like the *Pascha*, was split. Epiphany remained on January 6. In the East it remained the celebration of Jesus' baptism, while in western Europe it became the celebration of the visit of the wise men, who represented the manifestation of God to the Gentiles.

The other and newer festival, which in time came to

dominate the cycle, was Christmas. The first mention of December 25 as Jesus' birthday is A.D. 354, and there is evidence that this date may have been observed by Christians in Rome about 336 and in Africa prior to 312.

Both Christmas and Epiphany represent, as do developments in the Easter Cycle at the same time, the Christians' growing desire to celebrate the anniversaries of specific days in the life of Christ. The Bible says nothing to indicate the day of the year on which Jesus was either born or baptized, or on which the wise men visited him. It is possible that the dates of January 6 and December 25 may have originated in winter solstice celebrations. As Christianity became the established religion of the Roman Empire, Christmas served as the replacement for the pre-Christian Festival of the Unconquered Sun that marked the winter solstice. The theme of light conquering darkness has always been prominent in both Christmas and Epiphany. On the other hand, these dates may have been calculated using traditions regarding the date of Jesus' death and identifying the day of his death with that of his conception.

Christmas, like Easter, became not only a day but a season for celebrating the manifestation of God in Jesus Christ. Both the day and the season begin at sunset Christmas Eve, but the exact length of the season has varied from one tradition and denomination to another. "The Twelve Days of Christmas," celebrated by the song, take the season through January 5 (Twelfth Night) but do not include Epiphany. Today United Methodists, among others, extend the Christmas season through Epiphany to recover a unified Christmas-Epiphany season, which like the Easter-Pentecost season includes two great days and the time between.

In recent years both Roman Catholic and Protestant churches have been recovering the old emphasis on the baptism of Christ at Epiphany by celebrating the Sunday after January 6 as the Baptism of the Lord, while keeping Epiphany itself as the commemoration of the visit of the wise men.

As early as the late fourth century, Christians saw that Christmas-Epiphany needed a preparatory season comparable to what Lent was becoming in the Easter Cycle. This eventually became Advent as we know it, which begins on the fourth Sunday before Christmas and continues until sunset Christmas Eve. While penitence and spiritual discipline have sometimes been emphasized in Advent, as in Lent, the dominant note of the season has been hope and expectancy. The word *advent* means "coming." In Advent the church celebrates its hope and expectancy in the comings of Christ—past, present, and future. We identify with those in ancient Israel who looked for the coming of the Messiah, and we look forward to the yearly celebration of Christ's birth and manifestation. We look for the coming of Christ here and now through the power of the Holy Spirit. We look forward to Christ's coming in final victory.

How do you and your congregation celebrate the Christmas Cycle?

In most congregations Christmas is almost, but not quite, as high a point in the Christian year as Easter. Music and other arts have an especially large part in our worship during Advent and Christmas. The main emphasis is usually upon Sunday services, but festive services are commonly held on Christmas Eve and sometimes on Christmas Day as well.

There is a strong tendency for the Sundays after Christmas to be experienced as a letdown and for Advent to become the Christmas Season rather than the season preparatory to Christmas. In many United Methodist congregations, particularly those that do not hold Christmas Eve or Christmas Day services, the high point of the Christmas Cycle is "Christmas Sunday," the Fourth Sunday of Advent, the Sunday before Christmas.

There has been a strong movement in recent years to restore Advent as a preparatory season. Advent candles are lit, reminding us that Christmas is still to come. More Advent hymns are sung, especially during the earlier Sundays of Advent. If Christmas carols cannot be held back until Christmas Eve, they may at least be saved until the latter Sundays of Advent.

But the Christmas Cycle is by no means confined to churches. It is probably the biggest celebration of the year in most American homes and in the American society at large.

What is celebrated in our society at large as the Christmas season is a complex mixture of the Christian and the secular—Jesus' birthday and a midwinter festival. One need not be a Christian to dream of a white Christmas, sing of sleigh bells, set up a Christmas tree, exchange gifts and cards, or go to Christmas parties; but as Christians we can do all these things in the spirit of the Christ whose birth we celebrate. The secular Christmas season begins well before Advent, and in fact a large part of our preparation for Christmas consists of activities like shopping and sending cards and letters. These preparations can be as much or as little in the spirit of Christ as we choose to make them.

For most Christians in America, the Christmas Cycle is even more a home celebration than a church celebration. Advent and Christmas means shopping, setting up Christmas trees and other decorations, preparing and eating Christmas foods, family reunions, gift-giving rituals, reading or telling Christmas stories, and watching Christmas television specials. United Methodist congregations that have no Christmas Eve or Christmas Day services commonly urge that Christmas be observed by families at home. When

Christmas Day falls on a Sunday, attendance suffers because so many families choose to spend Christmas morning at home with their customary family ceremonies rather than attending church services.

Indeed, a major reason for the increase in recent years of Christmas Eve and Christmas Day services in United Methodist congregations is the growing number of persons who are not part of traditional nuclear families or who are unable to be with their families at Christmas, and who make church services their family Christmas celebrations.

Churches have become increasingly sensitive to the needs of the many persons for whom Christmas is a lonely time or for whom the season brings demands and strains that are hard to cope with. Ways are being found that enable persons to support one another at difficult times. Many persons invite others who cannot be with their families, or have no families, to join them for Christmas Eve or Christmas morning or Christmas dinner.

Where does this whole celebration of the Christmas Cycle lead so far as Christian commitment is concerned?

Many churches have an observance around New Year's or early in January for the renewal of our Christian covenant. It may be a Watchnight service. It may be the January service of Holy Communion. It may be the Sunday after January 6—the Baptism of the Lord—which is often observed as Covenant Sunday. Such a covenant service is an appropriate time for baptisms and for members of the whole congregation to renew their Christian covenant. It is a way of adapting the ancient tradition of Epiphany to modern America and bringing the Christmas Cycle to a fitting conclusion.

Through the Year

So far we have dealt with the high seasons of the Christian year, which have their origins in the first four centuries of

Christian history and which must be understood if we are to see the Christian year as a whole.

The profile of the Christian year has not only peaks and high plateaus but also plains and valleys. The parts of the Christian year that are not in the Christmas or Easter cycles are sometimes called *ordinary time.* We should not consider the word *ordinary* a put-down of these times in the year. Rather, it calls attention to the fact that the year is not one "high" after another but has a profile in which the high seasons are what they are because there are other seasons when there is a more steady, week-in, week-out feel to worship.

The Christian year begins on the First Sunday of Advent, and for the first few weeks that constitute the Christmas Cycle we have a very intense sense of what season it is in the Christian year.

Then comes the Season after Epiphany, which begins January 7 and lasts until Lent begins—sometime between February 4 and March 10. We are not particularly conscious of what season it is in the Christian year. Those of us who live in the north temperate zone of the earth are much more conscious of the fact that it is winter. Whether or not the weather is severe enough to reduce church attendance, this time tends to feel like a valley in the profile of the year—both in and out of church. However, this season is framed by two important observances. The first Sunday after Epiphany, as we have seen, is the Baptism of the Lord. The last Sunday after Epiphany is Transfiguration Sunday, on which we commemorate Jesus' transfiguration (Matthew 17:1-9; Mark 9:2-10; Luke 9:28-36; 2 Peter 1:17-18).

Then in the Easter Cycle, Christians tend again to be very conscious of what season it is in the Christian year.

The whole second half of the Christian year is the Season after Pentecost, which United Methodists may also call

Kingdomtide. It lasts from the day after Pentecost—sometime in May or June—until Advent begins the Christian year again. Once again we are not particularly conscious of what season it is in the Christian year.

In the north temperate zone of the earth, the weather and the rhythms of secular life make us conscious of the fact that it is summer and then fall. Summer may mean a slump, complete with choir vacation and guest preachers; or in recreational areas it may be the peak season with many visitors. "The busy fall season" is likely to feel like the beginning of the church year as congregations launch into fall programs.

Beginning with the first Sunday after Pentecost, which is Trinity Sunday, this time is full of special days and occasions. In the summer there are camps and conferences, outdoor services, and revival meetings. In the fall there is a host of days during which various church causes are promoted. This half of the year contains most of the major civil holidays in the United States; and if church attendance hits lows on Memorial Day, Fourth of July, and Labor Day weekends it is because so many persons are enjoying the time away from home with family and friends.

By November we are on an upward slope toward another high season, and these last few weeks of the Christian year are also a bridge to Advent and the new Christian year. Choirs are rehearsing Advent and Christmas music, Christmas programs are being prepared, and the world outside the church is already launching the Christmas season. A growing number of congregations celebrate All Saints' Day on the first day or the first Sunday of November, remembering the great parade of Christians through the ages who constitute the communion of saints. In congregations that follow the lectionary, the November readings center on the reign of Christ and lead up to the last Sunday of the Christian year—the festival of Christ the King (the Reign of Christ)—and then to Advent.

Thanksgiving in the United States, the fourth Thursday in November, is perhaps the one occasion in the year that most reflects our civil religion. It can be celebrated not only by Christians but by persons of other religions as well and is sometimes celebrated by interreligious services. It is also an important day for home religious rituals, often centering on Thanksgiving dinner and family reunions. Football games provide secular ritual. Churches may have their own or union services on Thanksgiving Day, Thanksgiving Eve, or Thanksgiving Sunday, at which thanks are given for the fruits of the earth, our heritage as an American people, or all of God's blessings.

Throughout the Christian year we are reminded of the day and season by bulletins and hymn boards, scriptures and sermons, hymns and anthems, prayers and acts of praise.

But it is by visuals that days and seasons may most immediately be announced—lilies at Easter and poinsettias at Christmas, chancel paraments and clergy stoles, banners and other hangings. While there is no universally accepted color code for the Christian year, United Methodists and many other Christians associate certain colors with particular days and seasons.

White and gold are considered joyous and festive colors and are used during the Christmas and Easter seasons and on other high days such as All Saints' Day.

Purple suggests both royalty and penitence and is used during Advent and Lent. Blue, the color of hope and of Mary the mother of Jesus, is also sometimes used during Advent.

Green as the color of growth is used after Epiphany and after Pentecost. During these periods of "ordinary time," white and red are often used on particular days when appropriate.

Red as the color of blood is often used during Holy Week and to commemorate martyrs. As the color of fire it is generally used on the day of Pentecost and may be used whenever the work of the Holy Spirit is emphasized. It may be used at evangelistic services, ordinations and consecrations, church anniversaries and homecomings, and civil holidays.

As we celebrate the changing days and seasons of the year, we can sanctify the time and let it teach us the things of God.

CHAPTER 10

Initiation and Passages

The Great Cycles and Beyond

The seasons recur year after year, but all years are not the same—just as the days and seasons of the year, the days of the week, the hours of the day, and the moments within an hour or within a worship service are not the same. Whenever we celebrate birthdays or anniversaries of any sort we answer the question, "What year is it?" The fact that we number our years A.D.—an abbreviation for *anno Domini,* which is Latin for "in the year of the Lord"—reminds us that it has been about two thousand years since the birth of Christ. At New Year's we may celebrate in our worship that we are entering a new and different "year of the Lord."

Anniversary services are a significant part of the worship of most churches. Congregations and entire denominations celebrate their fiftieth, hundredth, or two-hundredth anniversaries with appropriate services. Sometimes the celebration recalls an important episode in a congregation's history such as the erection of its present building; sometimes it commemorates a crucial event in our denominational history. Such celebrations tell us that the rhythms of time include even such great cycles as centuries. How will our second century compare with our first, or our third with our second?

Beyond even these great cycles, however, there are

passages in the life of a church or a person that will never recur. Once the passage is made, not only will that church or that person never be the same again, the passage itself cannot be repeated.

Baptism

In Christian worship the most basic of these rites of passage, as they are called, is baptism. Through baptism one is initiated not only into a congregation but also into the universal church—"grafted" as a new member into the body of Christ, marked and identified as a Christian disciple.

Baptism is as much a rite of passage for the church as it is for the person baptized. When a new member is joined to the body of Christ neither the member nor the body will ever be the same again. Candidates who are mature enough to make their own profession of faith take vows of commitment to Christ and the church. The church commits itself to nurture its new member through its worship, through church school classes and other nurturing groups, through pastoral care, and through the ongoing love and concern of the other members—regardless of whether the one being baptized is an infant or a mature adult. One or more sponsors, elder brothers and sisters in Christ, may agree to take special responsibilities for guiding and nurturing the one baptized. In the case of a child being baptized this responsibility is especially crucial and is normally assigned to the parent(s), although there may be other sponsors (godparents) as well. If the baptized person later becomes part of another congregation, that congregation recognizes the person as a baptized member of the universal church and assumes the appropriate nurturing responsibilities toward that person. Baptism is, therefore, an act of worship where both the congregation and the candidate—or the parent(s) or sponsor(s)—make solemn promises and accept solemn responsibilities.

Baptism has been basic to Christian worship since New Testament times. Jesus was baptized as the opening act of his public ministry (Matthew 3:13-17; Mark 1:9-11; Luke 3:21-22). We read in Matthew 28:19 that after his resurrection Jesus commanded the disciples to "make disciples of all nations, baptizing them in the name of the Father and of the Son and of the Holy Spirit." After Peter preached on the day of Pentecost, the day the church came into being, "those who welcomed his message were baptized, and that day about three thousand persons were added" (Acts 2:41).

Baptism itself is a washing with water, and like Holy Communion it is a basic human act through which God acts in our lives. Like Holy Communion, it is called a sacrament, and it is a mystery through which we participate in the mystery of the gospel. It means more than any explanation can tell us, and the many New Testament references to baptism describe its meanings through a variety of images. Each image shows one or more facets of baptism, but no one image shows us the whole meaning. We are baptized into union with Christ—into death, burial, and resurrection with Christ (Romans 6:3-5; Colossians 2:12). We are incorporated by baptism into one body, the church, in which we have put on Christ like a garment and are all one in Christ (1 Corinthians 12:13; Galatians 3:27-28). Baptism signifies being born anew of water and the Spirit (John 3:3-5; Titus 3:5). The cleansing action of water in baptism represents the forgiveness of sin (Acts 2:38; 22:16; 1 Corinthians 6:11; Hebrews 10:22; 1 Peter 3:21). Baptism represents the receiving of the Holy Spirit (Matthew 3:16; Mark 1:9-10; Luke 3:21-22; Acts 2:38; 19:1-7).

All these biblical images make it clear that baptism is a sign of what God does for us in Christ. God has taken the initiative in making covenant with us, and whatever we do in faith is always in response to what God has already done for us. The response of faith, however, is essential to making God's gifts effective in our lives.

It is unfortunate that baptism, which makes us one in Christ, has so often been the occasion of estrangement among Christians because of differing interpretations, each of which can claim support from one or more of the above images.

Exactly how should persons be totally immersed in the water, as suggested by the image of burial and resurrection with Christ? Should the water be poured or sprinkled on their heads, as suggested by the image of pouring out the Holy Spirit? Does immersion in flowing water suggest more of these images than immersion in still water? Perhaps it is best that baptism take place in a variety of such modes, so as to bring out the different facets of its rich imagery. The United Methodist Church gives candidates for baptism, or their parents, a choice of modes; and we may be glad that some persons choose one mode and others choose another mode.

A still deeper division among Christians concerns whether or not infants may be baptized.

Many Christians believe that infants cannot make the essential response of faith to what God has done for them, and that baptism should therefore be delayed until the candidate is able to make a public profession of faith. They also point out that nowhere is it explicitly stated that an infant was baptized.

The United Methodist Church, however, together with most Christians, holds that an infant who is part of a Christian household should be baptized. They point out that God's covenant with ancient Israel treated the family as a unit and that if God's new covenant through Christ had been different at this point the New Testament writers would surely have felt it necessary to make the difference clear—which they did not. On the contrary, Peter on the day of Pentecost clearly reinforces treating the family as a unit by saying: "Repent, and be baptized. . . . For the promise is to you and to your children" (Acts 2:38-39). Furthermore, when the head of a household made a profession of faith, the whole household was baptized (Acts 16:15, 33; 18:8; 1 Corinthians 1:16). We may assume that some of these households contained children too young to make a public profession of faith. If there is no explicit statement in the New Testament that an infant was baptized, neither is there a statement, or even a suggestion, that anyone born and raised in a Christian family made a profession of faith sometime in the course of growing up and was then baptized. Many believe that little children have their own form of faith, appropriate to their level of development if not yet expressed in thoughts and words; and Jesus' statement in Mark 10:13-16 is often quoted in this connection.

Regardless of the age of the person being baptized, we may say that the response of faith to what God has done is given by the whole congregation or even the whole universal church, to which total response the candidates and their parents or sponsors contribute what they can at their particular level of mental and spiritual development. Even candidates making their own professions of faith are in most cases "babes in Christ." No one can say, "My personal faith is good enough." We can all say, "*God's* grace—*God's* undeserved love—is good enough."

What happens in a service when there are baptisms?

Sometimes the rite of baptism is a fairly incidental part of a Sunday service, but increasingly churches are holding baptisms on occasions in the Christian year when the baptisms can be the focus of the service. Any Sunday during the Great Fifty Days lends itself to baptisms, especially Easter Day and the day of Pentecost. Where the ancient Easter Vigil has been revived, baptism finds what is perhaps its ideal setting. The Baptism of the Lord (Covenant Sunday) in January and All Saints' Day in November are also appropriate occasions.

How much preparation should there be for baptism?

The early church took such preparation very seriously. Candidates were often prepared for three years or more before baptism. We have seen that Lent originated as the time when candidates for baptism underwent their final "scrutinies" and that Lent became also a time of renewal for the whole church. Persons were given additional instruction and were nurtured following baptism.

If a new member is to be grafted into the body of Christ, then it is important both that the new member be suitable and prepared for the grafting and that the body also be prepared to accept and not reject the new member. The Easter Cycle is a particularly appropriate time for this process. If your church has a tradition of annual revival meetings or special evangelistic services at some other time of year, this may serve a similar purpose. In any case, the candidate for baptism or the parent(s) or sponsor(s) of a child to be baptized should be carefully prepared for such an important step. The congregation should not take it for granted that it can assimilate the new member but should be carefully prepared for this step, remembering that even the addition of a new baby imposes a heavy responsibility on the nurturing congregation.

Let us look at the rite of baptism itself as it is found in our hymnal in three forms on pages 32-49. You will notice that it consists of several acts.

There is the introductory statement about baptism by the pastor, followed by the presentation of candidates.

A renunciation of sin and profession of faith is made by the candidate or the candidate's parent(s) or sponsor(s) and supported by the congregation as a whole. These acts are sometimes called the vows.

The pastor may give thanks over the water, very much as the pastor at Holy Communion gives thanks over the bread and wine, recalling what God has done for us in Christ, invoking the action of the Holy Spirit, and praying for those being baptized.

Then the candidate is baptized with water "in the name of the Father, and of the Son and of the Holy Spirit" (Matthew 28:19). Since the water has great sign value, there is a growing trend when baptism is by pouring or sprinkling to use enough water that it can be seen as it is being used.

The pastor, joined by others if desired, then places hands on the head of the person just baptized and invokes the continuing work of the Holy Spirit (Acts 8:14-17).

Sometimes the ancient practice of anointing with oil is followed. The word *Christ* means "the anointed one," and anointing identifies the person with Christ.

Finally, it is fitting and traditional that those just baptized join the rest of the congregation in Holy Communion as the completion of their Christian initiation.

Baptism is part of a lifelong process. What it signifies with respect to union with Christ, incorporation into Christ's body, spiritual rebirth, forgiveness of sin, and receiving the Holy Spirit does not happen all at once, but over the course of a lifetime. Whether the candidate is an infant or an adult, baptism looks backward to the grace of God that anticipated the candidate's birth and has been present from the beginning of life. And it looks forward to all that God will do in the rest of that person's life and eternally. The repentance and faith professed at baptism are part of an ongoing and developing life of repentance and faith, both for the church and for the individual member. The forgiveness of sin that baptism signifies is not simply forgiveness for sins committed previously but a lifelong process of forgiveness for the sin of a lifetime. Having been baptized in and of itself never entitles anyone to say, "Now I'm saved and am going to heaven." Nor would we ever say of anyone just because that person has not been baptized that she or he is not saved.

In the course of this lifelong process there are other rites of passage that build upon baptism.

Other Professions and Reaffirmations

It is an essential and crucial step in the development of Christian faith when persons first profess for themselves the Christian faith. Churches carefully nurture their children and youth toward this step in Sunday school classes and commonly in special classes taught by the pastor or some other qualified person. While there is great variation in the age at which persons take this step, depending both on the expectations of the congregation and community and also on the personal readiness of the individual, congregations commonly find that most of those under their nurture are ready to profess their faith sometime in later childhood or in their early teens. If they have not already been baptized they make this profession at their baptism. If they are already baptized, the United Methodist Church provides the rite of confirmation, at which they publicly profess their faith in the presence of the congregation.

The term *confirmation* has three important meanings: (1) Candidates confirm their personal commitment by accepting for themselves the vows made at their baptism. (2) God reconfirms the covenant in Christ to those who were too young to understand it when they were baptized. (3) The congregation confirms these persons in their relationship to the family of Christ and in the ministries to which all Christians are commissioned by baptism.

This rite follows the same order as that of baptism in our hymnal (pages 32-39 or 45-49). It includes the candidates' renunciation of sin and profession of faith and also the laying of hands upon the candidates' heads with the invocation of the Holy Spirit.

There are other occasions when persons profess their faith in a new way. This can happen at any stage in a person's life, and the character of this profession will vary with the person's level of faith development. It can represent the deepening of a commitment already present, or the recovery of a commitment that had for a time been lost, or a new commitment. It may follow an experience that the person can tell about. Sometimes the person's life has been clearly, even radically, changed. At other times there seems to have been a steady growth toward the new stage of faith that the person now professes.

Churches often provide persons with the opportunity to tell about an experience or profess a new or deepened faith and commitment. This may be done during congregational worship or in some more informal and intimate setting. Persons may reaffirm their renunciation of sin and profession of faith and receive again the laying on of hands, as at confirmation.

Such witnessing and professing can be an important passage for the congregation as well as for the individual. This new faith and commitment can bring growth and power to the whole congregation. It may also require of the congregation some difficult soul-searching and patient nurture. Persons who have grown up in a congregation or participated actively in its life may say of their previous professions of faith, "I didn't know what I was doing." They may ask accusingly, "Why didn't you ever teach me this?" They may use words or a style of talking or practices that are unfamiliar or unacceptable to others in the congregation. A student home from college or studying for the ordained ministry may denounce the congregation for its real or imagined shortcomings. By bearing with such witnessing and being patient with persons who are struggling to incorporate new experiences into their ongoing lives and relationships, a congregation can grow in Christ while nurturing the growth of these persons.

Sometimes there is need for an act of reconciliation. Someone who has been estranged from the church, perhaps after a bad incident, faces the people and makes or receives needed apologies. Someone may want and need to say, "I don't know how you could have been so patient with me." Persons witnessing to a new Christian experience found outside the four walls of their church may feel estranged as they wonder, "How can I tell the folks back in my home congregation what has happened to me?" For a congregation to rise to such an occasion and affirm such persons may be a rite of passage for everyone concerned.

Sometimes events in the life of a congregation, its community, or the nation make a corporate service of repentance or reconciliation appropriate.

Healing services are held in many congregations, often with Holy Communion. What happens at these may be anything from radically life-changing to quietly supportive, depending on the moving of the Spirit. Through such services persons and congregations can grow in Christ.

There are passages in the history of a congregation that give opportunity for affirming in some new way its faith and ministry. A congregation is organized and holds its first worship service. Ground is broken, or a foundation stone is laid, for a new building. A church building is opened for worship, or its indebtedness is paid off. New furnishings or musical instruments or hymnals or robes are put into use. A final service is held in an old building that is to be razed or given over to other use. A congregation is disbanded, or two or more congregations are merged. The appointment or reappointment of a pastor is celebrated. There is a service of farewell to a pastor who is moving or retiring. Other church staff, church officers, boards and committees, choirs and instrumentalists, church school workers, and other volunteers may be installed or recognized and thanked.

Ordinations and Consecrations

It is a very special rite of passage when one or more persons are ordained or consecrated to particular lifetime ministries within the general ministry of all Christians. Most such services in the United Methodist Church are held, not in a local congregation but at Annual Conference. You may wish to attend such services, and in any case it is helpful to know what they are.

In The United Methodist Church we ordain deacons and elders. *Deacon* is a New Testament term meaning "servant" or "attendant" (Romans 16:1; Philippians 1:1; 1 Timothy 3:8-13; and perhaps Acts 6:1-7). It is the first ordination, and after a period of probation usually leads to a second ordination, that of *elder*. Elders are referred to many times in the New Testament.

Certain elders are eventually consecrated as *bishops*—a term translated from a New Testament Greek word meaning "overseer" (Philippians 1:1; 1 Timothy 3:1-7; Titus 1:7-9).

In recent years The United Methodist Church has consecrated certain other persons as diaconal ministers to serve in ministries such as Christian education or church music.

Baptism is the basic consecration to the work of Christian ministry, and all further ordinations and consecrations build upon the foundation of baptism. Jesus' great commission (Matthew 28:19-20) and the enabling power of the Holy Spirit (Acts 1 and 2) are not restricted to a group of professionals but were given to all Christians. The whole Letter to the Hebrews makes it clear that Christ alone is our high priest, and the First Letter of Peter tells baptized Christians that they are a priesthood (2:5, 9). Within this priesthood, or ministry, "there are varieties of gifts, but the same Spirit; and there are varieties of service, but the same Lord" (1 Corinthians 12:4-5). "[Christ's] gifts were that some should be apostles, some prophets, some evangelists, some pastors and teachers, to equip the saints for the work of ministry, for building up the body of Christ" (Ephesians 4:11-12). "The saints" in New Testament usage refers to the whole body of Christians, and it is the function of pastors, teachers, and others to use their special gifts and calling to equip the whole body for the work of ministry.

Our ordination and consecration services are services of the Word and sometimes include Holy Communion. A charge based upon scripture is given to the candidates, who then take vows. The act of ordination or consecration itself has as its visible sign the laying on of hands, with the invocation of the Holy Spirit. This recalls baptism and confirmation, and it signifies that it is not only the church but, ultimately, God who ordains. There may be other acts such as the giving of a Bible, chalice, or stole; but these are secondary to the laying on of hands with prayer. When Holy Communion concludes the service, the newly ordained or consecrated may take an appropriate role in addition to receiving communion.

Christian Marriage

Marriage among Christians may be solemnized—blessed or consecrated—in a service of Christian worship. While the marriages of early Christians were sometimes blessed during worship, it is only gradually over the centuries that this practice has come to be expected.

In the United States ordained clergy as well as certain civil magistrates are authorized agents of the state in officiating at legal marriages. Christians may choose to be married before a civil magistrate instead of an ordained Christian minister, and The United Methodist Church recognizes that such marriages are just as valid as those where clergy officiate. Marriages at which United Methodist clergy officiate are not always held in a church sanctuary or chapel, nor are they necessarily part of a service of worship. Often in marriages, acts of worship such as prayers are mixed with secular music and other symbolism not usually associated with worship.

Increasingly, United Methodists marry in a service of worship. This is most clearly seen in "A Service of Christian Marriage" on pages 864-69 of our hymnal. Here the marriage is part of a worship service that includes proclamation of the Word and may also include Holy Communion.

Marriage is transformed for Christians when it is based upon the foundation of baptism. As baptism grafts a new member into the body of Christ in a covenant relationship with God through Christ, so Christian marriage unites two persons into one flesh (Mark 10:8; Ephesians 5:28-31) in a marriage covenant modeled after our covenant relationship with Christ (1 Corinthians 11:2; Ephesians 5:21-33; Revelation 21:2).

Holy Communion on this occasion means not only that the couple begins their marriage by being joined in this climactic act of Christian worship (which is the acting out of our union with Christ), but also that they do this as part of the wider body of Christ, the communion of saints. For this reason not only the couple but also the others present should be invited to receive communion, even though for various reasons some may choose not to do so.

At any service of Christian marriage, persons present may be reminded of their own marriage covenants and may see these as being reaffirmed by their participation in the marriage of another couple.

In a service of worship couples may also publicly celebrate their wedding anniversary, reaffirm their marriage covenant, or (if they were married in a civil ceremony) affirm their existing marriage for the first time in the covenantal context of Christian worship.

Christian Funerals and Memorial Services

The final passage in life is death. From time immemorial human beings have expressed themselves in ritual when someone dies.

When Christians die their families and friends almost always request some type of funeral or memorial service that is an act of Christian worship. This is usually conducted by an ordained Christian minister, although laypersons occasionally conduct funerals or memorial services, and secular organizations often conduct rites before or after the service. The traditional funeral is a rite conducted in the presence of the body of the deceased, after which the body is committed to its final resting place, usually burial in the earth. A memorial service is conducted in the absence of the body, either instead of or in addition to a funeral.

Where the funeral or memorial service is a Christian service of worship, it is traditionally based upon the foundation of baptism. It includes a Service of the Word, and sometimes Holy Communion. "A Service of Death and Resurrection" on pages 870-75 of our hymnal is such a service.

The Christian gospel is a message of death and resurrection—Christ's and ours. Jesus spoke of his own death, burial, and resurrection as a baptism (Mark 10:38-39; Luke 12:50) in which his disciples were to share, and Paul tells us that in baptism we are buried and raised with Christ (Romans 6:4; Colossians 2:12). Death no longer has dominion over Christ, and if we have died with Christ we believe we shall also live with him (Romans 6:8-9). For the Christian, "to live is Christ, and to die is gain" (Philippians 1:21). Committal of the deceased to God and of the body to its final resting place recalls the act of baptism and derives its Christian meaning from God's baptismal covenant with us.

Traditionally in a Christian funeral the committal is preceded—or occasionally in modern practice followed—by a Service of the Word. A Christian memorial service is usually a Service of the Word. Scripture is read, interspersed with prayer and praise. There is commonly preaching that includes both a message from scripture and personal reference to the deceased. It is fitting that the funeral or memorial service of a Christian be held in the church, but it is often held in a funeral home or special chapel, or occasionally in the home of the deceased.

The character of funerals and memorial services varies with the circumstances of the deceased and of the mourners, but it is typically a mixture of mourning and

Christian affirmation. We acknowledge the reality of death, the pain of our loss, and the inevitability of our own death. We give thanks for the life that was lived and shared with us. We give praise that the one we have loved is eternally safe in God's love, which is also our own hope and security. We worship in the awareness that our gathering includes, invisibly, the whole communion of saints—that in Christ the circle is unbroken.

Holy Communion so wonderfully signifies all of this that it is most appropriate at Christian funerals and memorial services. Sometimes (as shown in the service in our hymnal) the funeral or memorial service itself is a full Service of Word and Table. Sometimes the pastor makes Holy Communion the focus of a call upon the family shortly after the funeral. The common meal in which family and perhaps friends so often join on the day of the funeral may have some of this same significance, and to make this evident it is possible to have Holy Communion under the pastor's leadership before such a meal.

The Ultimate Vision

Beyond the cycles of time and the passages of human life is the endless circle of eternity. The earthly lifetime of an individual comes to an end one day, but the gift of God is eternal life in Christ. Congregations and denominations, communities and nations also come one day to their end; but the communion of saints is eternal in God's love. The New Testament speaks repeatedly of "the ages" (eons)— "this age," "the close of the age," and "the age to come"—but tells us that the immortal God is "King of the ages." The Christ who will come in final victory at the end of the age will bring all who are in Christ into the glory of that victory. We are given the vision of a new heaven and a new earth, after the first heaven and the first earth have passed away. We are told that there will be no temple there, for even our churches and our services of worship will have had their time and ceased to be, in the presence of the God who will be "all in all."

Meanwhile, we have "the assurance of things hoped for, the conviction of things not seen." Every morning when we rise from sleep to a new day, every Lord's Day when we gather and the rhythm of call and response leads to the consummation of Holy Communion, whenever in the cycle of the seasons we pass through Good Friday and keep the feast of Easter, and when we celebrate death and resurrection in the passages of life, we anticipate the consummation of all things—the ultimate communion. And we know that all will be well.

For Further Reading

The United Methodist Hymnal: Book of United Methodist Worship. Nashville: The United Methodist Publishing House, 1989. The basic book of United Methodist worship.

Hickman, Hoyt L., Volume Editor. *The Worship Resources of The United Methodist Hymnal.* Nashville: Abingdon Press, 1989. An introduction to the worship services and Psalter in the hymnal.

————. *Workbook on Communion and Baptism.* Nashville: Discipleship Resources, 1990. For individual or class study of the meanings of Holy Communion and baptism.

Sanchez, Diana, Volume Editor. *The Hymns of The United Methodist Hymnal.* Nashville: Abingdon Press, 1989. An introduction to the hymns, canticles, and acts of worship in the hymnal.

Stookey, Laurence Hull. *Baptism: Christ's Act in the Church.* Nashville: Abingdon Press, 1982. A comprehensive study of baptism.

White, James F. *Introduction to Christian Worship* (Revised Edition). Nashville: Abingdon Press, 1990. A comprehensive introduction to Christian worship.

————. *Sacraments as God's Self Giving.* Nashville: Abingdon Press, 1983. A comprehensive study of the meanings of baptism and Holy Communion.

Willimon, William H. *Remember Who You Are.* Nashville: The Upper Room, 1980. A popular study of baptism.

————. *Sunday Dinner*. Nashville: The Upper Room, 1981.
A popular study of Holy Communion.

————. *With Glad and Generous Hearts*. Nashville: The Upper
Room, 1986. A popular study of Sunday worship.